PUBLISHED BY BOOM BOOKS

www.boombooks.biz

ABOUT THE SERIES

.... But after that, I realised that I knew very little about these parents of mine. They had been born about the start of the Twentieth Century, and they died in 1970 and 1980. For their last 50 years, I was old enough to speak with a bit of sense.

I could have talked to them a lot about their lives. I could have found out about the times they lived in. But I did not. I know almost nothing about them really. Their courtship? Working in the pits? The Lock-out in the Depression? Losing their second child? Being dusted as a miner? The shootings at Rothbury? My uncles killed in the War? Love on the dole? There were hundreds, thousands of questions that I would now like to ask them. But, alas, I can't. It's too late.

Thus, prompted by my guilt, I resolved to write these books. They describe happenings that affected people, real people. The whole series is, to coin a modern phrase, designed to push your buttons, to make you remember and wonder at things forgotten. The books might just let nostalgia see the light of day, so that oldies and youngies will talk about the past and re-discover a heritage otherwise forgotten. Hopefully, they will spark discussions between generations, and foster the asking and answering of questions that should not remain unanswered.

BORN IN 1946?

WHAT ELSE HAPPENED?

RON WILLIAMS

AUSTRALIAN SOCIAL HISTORY

BOOK 8 IN A SERIES OF 35
FROM 1939 to 1973

War Babies Years (1939 to 1945):   7 Titles
Baby Boom Years (1946 to 1960):   15 Titles
Post Boom Years (1961 to 1973:   13 Titles

BOOM, BOOM BABY, BOOM

Published by Boom Books.
Wickham, NSW, Australia

Web: www.boombooks.biz
Email: jen@boombooks.biz

Creator: Williams, Ron, 1934 - author

ISBN: 9780987543691 (paperback)

© 2015.   This printing 2023.
Series: Born in series, book 8.
Australia--History--Miscellanea--20th century.
Dewey Number: 994.04

Cover image: National Archives of Australia

A1200, L2308, Neil Harvey Australian cricketer;
A1200, L79, Correspondence school student;
A1200, L7788, steam train;
A1200, L3500, smoko;
M1409, 31 B, PM Ben Chifley (centre) with Doc Evatt and Clement Attlee.

TABLE OF CONTENTS

IMPORTANT PEOPLE AND EVENTS

King of England	George VI
Prime Minister of Oz	Ben Chifley
Leader of Opposition	Bob Menzies
Governor General	Duke of Gloucester
The Pope	Pius XII
US President	Harry Truman
PM of Britain (after April)	Clement Attlee

HOLDER OF THE ASHES:

Since 1938	England
1946-7	Australia 3 - 0
1948	Australia 4 - 0

MELBOURNE CUP WINNERS:

1945	Rainbird
1946	Russia
1947	Hiraji

ACADEMY AWARDS, 1946:

Best Actor	Frederic March
Best Actress	Olivier de Havilland
Best Movie	Years of our Lives

PREFACE TO THIS SERIES

This book is the 8th in **a series** of books that I have researched and written. It tells a story about a number of important or newsworthy Australia-centric events that happened in 1946. The **series** covers each of the years from 1939 to 1973, for a total of 35 books.

I developed my interest in writing these books a few years ago at a time when my children entered their teens. My own teens started in 1947, and I started trying to remember what had happened to me then. I thought of the big events first, like Saturday afternoon at the pictures, and cricket in the back yard, and the wonderful fun of going to Maitland on the train for school each day. Then I recalled some of the not-so-good things. I was an altar boy, and that meant three or four Masses a week. I might have thought I loved God at that stage, but I really hated his Masses. And the schoolboy bullies, like Greg Fannell, and the hapless Freddie Ebans. Yet, to compensate for these, there was always the beautiful, black headed, blue-sailor-suited June Brown, who I was allowed to worship from a distance.

I also thought about my parents. Most of the major events that I lived through came to mind readily. But after that, I realised that I really knew very little about these parents of mine. They had been born about the start of the Twentieth Century, and they died in 1970 and 1980. For their last 20 years, I was old enough to speak with a bit of sense. I could have talked to them a lot about their lives. I could have found out about the times they lived in. But I did not. I know almost nothing about them really. Their courtship? Working in the pits? The Lock-out in the Depression? Losing their second child? Being dusted as a miner? The shootings at Rothbury?

My uncles killed in the War? There were hundreds, thousands of questions that I would now like to ask them. But, alas, I can't. It's too late.

Thus, prompted by my guilt, I resolved to write these books. They describe happenings that affected people, real people. In **1946,** there is some coverage of international affairs, but a lot more on social events within Australia. This book, and the whole series is, to coin a modern phrase, designed to push the reader's buttons, to make you remember and wonder at things forgotten. The books might just let nostalgia see the light of day, so that oldies and youngies will talk about the past and re-discover a heritage otherwise forgotten. Hopefully, they will spark discussions between generations, and foster the asking and the answering of questions that should not remain unanswered.

The sources of my material. I was born in 1934, so that I can remember well a great deal of what went on around me from 1939 onwards. But of course, the bulk of this book's material came from research. That meant that I spent many hours in front of a computer reading electronic versions of newspapers, magazines, Hansard, Ministers' Press releases and the like. My task was to sift out, **day-by-day**, those stories and events that would be of interest to the most readers. Then I supplemented these with materials from books, broadcasts, memoirs, biographies, government reports and statistics. And I talked to old-timers, one-on-one, and in organised groups, and to Baby Boomers about their recollections. People with stories to tell came out of the woodwork, and talked no end about the tragic, and funny, and commonplace events that have shaped their lives.

The presentation of each book. For each year covered, the end result is a collection of short Chapters on many of the topics that concerned ordinary people in that year. I think I have covered most of the major issues that people then were interested in. On the other hand, in some cases I have dwelt a little on minor frivolous matters, perhaps to the detriment of more sober considerations. Still, in the long run, this makes the book more readable, and hopefully it will convey adequately the spirit of the times.

Each of the books is mainly Sydney based, but I have been **deliberately national in outlook**, so that readers elsewhere will feel comfortable that I am talking about matters that affected them personally. After all, housing shortages and strikes and juvenile delinquency involved **all** Australians, and other issues, such as problems overseas, had no State component in them. Overall, I expect I can make you wonder, remember, rage and giggle equally, no matter where you hail from.

SOME EVENTS FROM 1945

Much of this book, **1946**, is still talking about the leftovers from the War. That is because wartime regulations and rationing, and wartime governmental controls were still in place. Hundreds of thousands of troops were still in the Armed Forces, waiting to be demobbed. There were still 3,000 **Japanese** soldiers in POW camps here, waiting to be repatriated. Jobs were short, money was short, housing was very short – all because of the War. Everywhere, austerity was still the official cry of government. So 1946 was the year when every man and woman blinked at the light and began the multi-year fight to be free of the legacy of the War. This battle continued for a full decade; but in 1946, the thinking of the Australian population was dominated by the very slow retreat from an entrenched military footing.

First, however, we should look more closely at 1945. On August 15, 1945, Japan agreed to the unconditional surrender that had been secretly on and off the table since the beginning of the year. The military forces of that once-great nation had suffered defeat after defeat, the navy had been almost completely destroyed, and Tokyo and other major cities had been fire-bombed nightly for months. Then the United States put an end to all chances of a glorious revival, one last desperate counter-attack, by dropping atomic bombs on Nagasaki and Hiroshima. The complete destruction of these two major cities squashed any thoughts of a comeback, and it was obvious that even worse destruction was inevitable if resistance persisted. So, on August 15, Emperor Hirohito took to the airwaves in Japan and solemnly, with immense sadness, admitted total defeat and told his nation to lay down all arms.

For Australians, the too-good-to-be-true cessation of war was wonderful. They had not expected it just then. They had been told just a few days earlier of the dropping of two atom bombs. But, in a nation that had grown weary of the lies of war-time censorship and propaganda, they had spent little time worrying about the significance of these bombs. So, to wake early one Wednesday morning and to find that the War was over, was the greatest news that many of them ever had.

What a relief it was for all. For the mums and dads, and wives and lovers, and families and friends, and for everyone, the nation thanked God that no more Australian sons or daughters would be killed or maimed, or enslaved in concentration camps. The rejoicing was tinged with the great sorrow that everyone felt for the fallen heroes and their nearest and dearest, and with a great sense of loss that time would scarcely diminish. Yet the nation was focused on that day with thoughts of peace, peace, and more peace. "Our boys" – and girls – would be back for Christmas, and Mothers' Day and Melbourne Cup Day. They would be Home. Here. Huggable.

For the wartime stay-at-homes, there would be no more sleeping in air-raid shelters in the suburbs round Sydney and Newcastle harbours, waiting for another attack from Japanese submarines. No more air-raids on Darwin that took 80 lives. No more slit trenches and shelters that were dug in every school ground in the nation. No more of any of this. Even the railway stations would be able to display their names again. And men's shirt tails would be longer than the four inches that was mandated by wise and caring governments during the War. But overriding all this, people were thankful, many of them to God, that carnage had stopped, that everyone was free from terrible fears, and that the world would now return to the sanity that peace just might bring.

On the eve of the 1946 New Year, Australians were hopeful. They wanted and expected something better than they had had in the past. They were not at all certain what it was that they wanted, and they knew not how to get it. They were still living with all sorts of austerities, and housing shortages, and war-time rules and regulations. They were confronted by governments that were all broke and in dire financial difficulties, and who had the task of turning a war-time economy back to peace. They were just starting to learn that the rigidities in society, previously accepted, were no longer necessary, that the days of deep subjugation to England were over, and that the old social strata and structures were weakened almost beyond salvage.

So, indeed, they were hopeful. They expected that things would change for the better quickly. In this, they were disappointed. Believe it on not, in this great pasture that we call Australia, butter stayed rationed until 1952. But gradually, in fits and starts, things did improve. If we look ahead to 1968 – the last year in this series of 30 books – we can hardly recognise the nation. Most of the changes were, I believe, for the better.

New Year's Day. But now, we are at the start of 1946. On the Eve, parties were held throughout the nation in just about every home. In Sydney, the pleasure-chasing masses in those days celebrated in run-down and grubby Kings Cross, amid the nightclubs, prostitutes, crooked cops, and drunks. At midnight, there was "dancing in the streets" and "a cacophony of whistles" that apparently went on for almost a minute. Two hours later, it was reported in the *Newcastle Herald* that it was "business as usual."

Next morning, there were very sober editorials in each of the major dailies. They had a common theme. The world is now at peace, "the guns have ceased to thunder, and killing is no longer the principal pre-occupation of mankind." We have escaped from the tyranny of hateful dictators and the cruelty of wicked oppressors because the forces of right triumphed, as they always will, over the forces of evil. "Even the most heedless reveller" last night was fully aware that this blessed escape came with the terrible loss of millions of lives and the destruction of the dreams of millions more, but at the same time, was aware that the world was now filled with hopes that could only be realized in a world where peace prevailed.

It was stirring stuff, as it should have been. New Year's Day is often a day for reflection, on the past and the future. These editorials touched people right round the nation, and are still remembered by many, with intense relief, as signalling that the War was really over. One lady in St Kilda told me she read the editorial in *The Age*, and started to cry. She had not cried since the night that War was declared, when she realised that her son Tom could be called to serve. All through the next six years, even when Tom was reported Killed in Action in France, she had not cried. Now, reading the editorial, she cried. For six hours, she remembered Tom and the fears she had for him every minute of the day. She cried for the lost ones of relatives and friends. She cried for her family that had suffered the loss of Tom. All of a sudden, the grief she had been bottling up came out. And when it was out, she said, "I felt that a burden was gone. I dropped to my knees and thanked God for all my blessings, for all the things I still had left."

Another lady, who worked in a munitions factory at Lithgow during the War, talked about her Victory Garden. From about 1942 onwards, people were encouraged to grow a small plot of vegetables in their backyards so that some of the national demand for food would be met from this source. This lady had her husband dig such a plot. Then she went to it on the first day, all by herself, and "beat hell out of it with a Dutch hoe." She explained to me that she was fed up with the violence and hatred in the world. All she wanted to do was bring up her children and love her husband in peace. One of her sons had been killed, and two others were still over there. So, on that day, she vented her anger on the poor, unsuspecting plot. And she did this off and on through the war, though most times she just raked and dug. But "some days, it got too much for me again, and I flogged that plot till it screamed for mercy".

That little garden never grew a single veggie. Not even a weed survived the battering. Then, on New Year's Day, 1946, she sat down and reminisced about everything that mattered. She slowly decided that her two dead sons would want her to get on with her life and that the new hope abroad in the nation was there for her too. That very day, she symbolically got some horse dung, dug it into the garden, and planted some poppy seeds. She knew that sowing poppies then was completely out of season, "but I just wanted some red poppies in my garden".

The editorials went on to say that it would take years "before the worst of the world's wounds are healed, and the stricken people are able to turn to the task of reconstruction". The time to start was now. This nation had not suffered as Europeans and British had suffered, and would soon have ample supplies of everything. "If we gird our loins up, and all pull together, we can speedily repair the damages that we have suffered".

The Governor General's message was full of sadness for the past and hope for the future. The Duke of Gloucester was a great representative of the Queen on ceremonial occasions, and his speeches were equal to the best for the number and variety of platitudes he carefully and peachily enunciated. "In the War, the Commonwealth's contribution to victory was glorious and splendid.... In the peace, its share must be equally fine if we are to build a better happier world." He ended with a flourish of words that even now make me want to jump to my feet, wave a flag, and sing "God Save the King".

"From personal experience, I know that in Australia, loyalty to the Crown, and the spirit of service are second to none anywhere in the Empire. Therefore, with high purpose, go forward to the New Year resolved to do your part to the glory of God, and for the benefit of the Empire and the world."

The Duke and Duchess left Australia towards the end of 1946. This, to me, signalled the beginning of a significant change in this nation's attitude to the monarchy. Because at that time, there were many voices raised **to appoint an Australian** to the GG position. Remember that back then, loyalty to the Crown was universal. In England, there was an official legal creed that "the King cannot commit a crime." In our land, 12,000 miles from England, the reverence for Royalty was preserved intact. For example, every person stood at the start of picture shows and made some sort of noise while our national anthem (God Save the King) was played. And apart from public symbols such as this, there was privately here a deep respect right across the nation for the person of the King and his family.

Yet, when the Duke left, many Letters to the newspapers were insistent that the next GG should be Australian. As it turned out, the position **did** go to the local boy William McKell, the recently-retired Premier of NSW. Here we have something of an anomaly. This nation was as loyal as can be to the British monarchy, and to the British Empire, yet now it wanted and accepted one of its own as the representative of the King. It was one of the first post-war signs of an attitude that grew and grew over the next half century, and which saw Australia move away from allegiance to Britain, and then saw us put our trust (of a sort) into America, and ultimately get close to a republic that had completely severed all ties to the monarchy. This is a process that this series of books will follow with interest as the years roll on.

So, with this brief introduction we are ready for 1946. Just before that, I will give you **a few Rules** that I use in writing.

MY RULES IN WRITING

NOTE. Throughout this book, I rely a lot on re-producing Letters from the newspapers. Whenever I do this, I put the text in a different font, and indent it a little, and make the font somewhat smaller. **I do not edit the text at all**. That is, I do not correct spelling or grammar, and if the text gets at all garbled, I do not correct it. It's just as it was seen in the Papers.

SECOND NOTE. The material for this book, when it comes from newspapers, is reported as it was seen at the time. If the benefit of hindsight over the years changes things, then I **might** record that in my **Comments**. The info reported thus reflects matters **as they were seen in 1946.**

THIRD NOTE. Let me also apologise in advance to anyone I might offend. In a work such as this, it is certain some people will think I got some things wrong. I am sure that I did, but please remember, all of this is **only my opinion**. And really, **my opinion does not matter one little bit in the scheme of things.** I hope you will say "silly old bugger", and shrug your shoulders and read on.

Now, we *are* ready to go. Fasten your seatbelts.

JANUARY NEWS ITEMS

January 1st. **Hitler's will was discovered**. He talked about how he intended to commit suicide with his lady-friend Eva Braun. That is what he eventually did, and the detail of the will is said to **lay to rest all the rumours** that said his death had been faked, and that **he would arise again** and lead his armies to greater glory....

He ended his will with the hope that after his death, the **peasants and workers would not give up** "but would continue on with our great cause that will grow some day to a **glorious re-birth of our National Socialist movement**."

A strike by steelworkers ended early in the New Year. This strike **was a big one, and lasted for 16 weeks**. As a result, metal workers and associated trades, and drivers, and shippers had become short of materials to work on. Now that the strike was over, it was expected that **200,000 displaced workers would resume work immediately, and another 200,000 within a fortnight....**

This strike was called to get pay increases for workers. The **steelworkers were controlled by the Communists** who were quite happy to do as much damage as possible to the nation's economy. **We will hear more from the Reds later.**

Famous English comedian **Stan Laurel**, now living in Hollywood **has had a few interesting years**. He married in the mid-1930's, and divorced in 1938. He married another woman, but decided that he wanted to re-marry his first wife. So he divorced his second bride. He re-married, but now his current wife wants a second divorce. Apparently, he will now have **three lots of alimony to pay**.

The **new wonder drug, penicillin**, that was so effective in healing injuries during the war, will now be used in **treating bronchitis.** Sprayed on a sore throat, it will cure an infection within 24 hours. It has no value against common colds, but **will stop a thick-running nose** in its tracks.

Holiday makers were returning to the capital cities. **Transport for them was in serious short supply....**

For example, at the NSW regional city of Newcastle, the Station Master was assaulted three times and his trousers were torn away when a train carrying 800 people pulled into his station on its way to Sydney. 700 people were waiting on the platform for the train, which **was already over-loaded**. The Station Master suffered his hurts when he tried to control the chaos that ensued. **Similar scenes were occurring all over the nation.**

Army disposal stores were appearing in every one of our nation's cities. These were selling **materials that the army no longer needed**. This included thousands of tons of clothing, netting, mosquito sticks, crib tins, tinned food, clothing, and boots....

It is possible to **buy a .303 rifle** and hundreds of bullets without any questions asked....

At a different level, **serious bits of military hardware were being discarded**. For example, trucks and tanks. And **300 planes** that were a year ago considered as essential to Australia's defence, are now to be dumped at sea. They are now considered as "surplus, obsolete, and of no value to anyone." Their initial cost was seven million Pounds.

WHAT MIGHT 1946 BRING?

Our military men were coming back into circulation. What were their expectations?

First and foremost, they could expect that loads of soldiers would get out of uniform. Half the army was still stuck overseas on Occupation duties, or in barracks in Australia, waiting for their turn to be released. Then, they could expect these men would get the jobs that had been promised them, and find a comfy place to live. They might even find some nice girls, and settle down to married life in the suburbs.

There was a lot of talk about hunger overseas, and refugees, and this might become a bit of a worry. There was also the thought that this nation had run up a big deficit during the war, and **that** would have to be repaid. But none of this was pressing, and if it got serious we could handle it.

One worry was that the war finished about four months ago, but as yet rationing of everything was still in place. Hopefully, this will go in the next few months. Then again, there had been no housing built during the war, so finding that comfy place to live might be a bit of a problem. And maybe they might not **want** their old jobs back, and might want to try something different.

One thing was certain, some of **the old rules and strictures** that bedevilled them pre-war would never again slow them down as they had pre-war. As for problems, they had just beaten the Japs, so could doubtless handle any other matters that cropped up. So, **they are ready**, **ready for 1946**, knowing full well that the brave new world was here **now**, and **now** was the time to enjoy it in this land of powdered milk and no honey.

LORD HAW HAW (WILLIAM JOYCE)

William Joyce was an American, born of two English parents in Brooklyn in April 1906. As a young child, he migrated to Ireland with his parents, where he attended a Catholic primary school, with his later education coming from the Jesuits. An interesting start to life, you might say, perhaps a bit out of the ordinary, but nothing really spectacular. But 40 years after his birth, his departure from life was quite spectacular, because on January 3rd, 1946, he was executed at Wandsworth prison, by order of the British government, for treason. His crime was that **he had broadcast pro-Nazi propaganda from Germany to Britain,** virtually from the start of the War in 1939 until its end in 1945.

At the age of 17 in London, he joined up with fascist groups, at a time when Mussolini was moving from strength to strength with his own Fascism in Italy. For the next 15 years, he developed his anti-semitism, he appeared on platforms with the famous or infamous Sir Oswald Mosely, and ultimately formed his own breakaway Fascist party in 1937. Before the outbreak of war, fearing that he would be interned if he stayed in Britain, he went to Germany in early September 1939.

It took him only two weeks to find a job. He was recruited as a foreign language broadcaster with the Ministry of Propaganda, headed by Dr Josef Goebbels. His job was to send short-wave radio messages – from Hamburg – into enemy territories, with the intention of lowering morale within the general public and the armed forces. He set about this with gusto, and soon became a popular star of evening radio in Britain. His raucous voice assailed the air as he spoke with a hint of majesty, with an air of complete superiority sometimes mixed with a modicum of pity for the downtrodden English masses.

He became known throughout Britain – and Australia – as Lord Haw Haw, and earned the honour of becoming one of the most hated persons in the English-speaking world.

His themes for the general public were that living conditions in England were shoddy and were markedly inferior to those in Germany, and that they were getting worse every day. He kept emphasising British unemployment, and contrasted it to you-know-where. For the servicemen, in Britain and wherever they might be, he gave statistics of how badly they were being mauled, of how hopeless their resistance was, and of how efficient and machine-like the German military was. At one stage, he was even able to override the BBC announcers who were giving out their own propaganda, and correct the casualty figures that the announcer had just uttered. The theme he developed over and over again was that defeat for Britain was inevitable, and in fact, just round the corner. Resistance was futile and costing lives and the resources of all concerned.

The British people listened. The BBC estimated in early **1940** that "Germany Calling" had an audience of **six million who listened every day or every second day**, another 18 million occasional listeners, and only 11 million who did not enjoy the broadcasts at all.

After 1940, his popularity dropped somewhat, but still he remained very important for the German war effort. So much so that in September 1944, he was awarded the German Cross of War Merit, First Class. This was a civil award, equivalent to an OBE, signed personally by the Fuhrer himself.

Why did they listen? It seems that one important reason is that German reports were right up to date, whereas the BBC and official military reports were often days behind. People knew that things were going on, and they reckoned that if they were being starved of information by the British officials, then they were better off getting some idea from the admittedly biased reports offered by the Germans. Then in a day's time, they could put that all together with the equally biased reports from Britain, and perhaps get some sort of realistic picture. As time went on, more and more listeners tuned in to scoff; his initial message was losing its effectiveness for them, because it was too clearly propaganda laid on with a heavy hand. But others - probably a small minority after a while - listened from fear that all he said was true.

There were suggestions during the war that the government should take some action to curtail Lord Haw Haw's influence. Systematic jamming of the broadcasts might do the trick. Or there might be a point-by-point rejoinder to him by the British. But for some reason, such measures were not adopted. Various government campaigns were of dubious value. For example, in July 1940, there was the release of the "What do I do campaign" with the following advertisement:

> What do I do if I come across a German broadcast when tuning my wireless? I say to myself that this blighter wants me to listen to him. Am I going to do what he wants? I remember that nobody can trust a word that he says, so I switch him off.

He gave his last broadcast to Britain on April 30, 1945, and was captured on May 28th.

EXCERPTS FROM HAW HAW

6th August, 1940. Waiting for the invasion.   I make no apology for saying again that invasion is certainly coming soon, but what I want to impress upon you is that nothing you can do is really of the slightest use. Don't be deceived by this lull before the storm, because, although there is still the chance of peace, Hitler is aware of the political and economic confusion in England, and is only waiting for the right moment. Then, when his moment comes, he will strike, and strike hard at the people whom Churchill has condemned to ruin in his crazy and fantastic plan to blockade Europe.

17th October, 1940. At the height of the bombing. All your daily social relationships are overthrown; people are deprived of sleep, and in many cases of food. Gas, electricity and water supplies are interrupted. You are being reduced to a primitive and nomad condition of subsistence. It is expected that pestilence and plague will break out. Every one of your cities will be wiped out. Existence in this country is bound up with industry. The land cannot feed one quarter of the population.

Do you intend to wait until your last machinery has been put out of action, before considering whether it would not be wiser to make peace. This great population of 50 millions will find itself without means of subsistence. People will starve by the millions. Pestilence will creep through the land, and no means will remain of creating order out of chaos.

You must summon up both courage and common sense, dismiss from office the corrupt and incompetent politicians, and save yourselves by demanding peace, as a whole people, which has been governed too long by rulers without conscience.

22nd November, 1940. After Coventry was bombed. Coventry is the most important place in England for the manufacture of aeroplane motors and such like. One bright night about 500 German aeroplanes flew over Coventry. They dropped about 1,000,000 lbs. of bombs. If you have any imagination at all, you can imagine what kind of a hell they let loose in Coventry that night. It was the worst hell that mankind can imagine. And that went on almost the whole night through. When dawn came there was nothing left but one pile of rubbish. The factories were gone altogether. Coventry will manufacture no more engines for months and months to come. It was the heaviest blow for British industry. Even Americans express their doubts after Coventry, as to whether England can last much longer.

31st December, 1942. As the Russians had victories. As the year draws to a close we are witnessing the dramatic spectacle of the Soviet Union dissipating its forces, squandering its reserves and smashing its war potential to pieces on the adamant rock of German resistance.

The extent of the enemy's sacrifices has been colossal and cannot be maintained. In the Stalingrad Sector, above all, the Soviets have been employing heavy forces and their losses have been proportionately high. Day after day, more Soviet tank losses have been reported and at the same time, the ratio between the German and Soviet air losses is incomparably in favour of the Luftwaffe. For example, it was reported yesterday that **sixty-seven Soviet aircraft had been shot down as against four German losses**; on Tuesday, the ratio was fifty-two to one in our favour. As might be expected, the Luftwaffe's superiority has dealt a hard blow at the enemy and it is now reported that the Soviets are being compelled to use untrained personnel in their larger bombers.

3rd February, 1943. The Germans defeated in Stalingrad. So far as divisions, brigades and battalions are concerned, Stalingrad **was** a German defeat. **But** when a Great Power like the National Socialist Reich is waging a total war, divisions and battalions can be replaced. If we review the position in sober and cold calculations, all sentiment apart, we must realise that the fall of Stalingrad cannot impair the German defensive system as a whole.

Whatever individuals have lost, whatever they may have sacrificed, there is nothing in the position as a whole to controvert the view that the main objectives of the enemy offensives have been frustrated. Stalingrad was a part of the price which had to be paid for the salvation of Europe from the Bolshevik hordes.

24th June, 1944. Hitler's last stand, the V-rockets. London and southern England have now been under bombardment for more than a week. For nine days, with very little interruption, the V-1 projectiles have been descending on the British capital.

The emergence of V-1 has provided a surprise for Germany's enemies and I believe they will have several other surprises "before the autumn leaves fall." Germany's military policy in this war is based not on slogging and on squandering, but upon a scientific economy and application of energy.

It can reasonably be assumed that the battle in the East against the Bolshevik foes of civilisation will be hard and fierce, and there is every reason to believe that the battle in the West against the capitalist agents of Jewish international finance will attain a climax of violence possibly without precedence. But in the closing rounds of this war, it will be seen that Germany has conserved her strength to a degree that will confound her enemies.

Haw Haw's vast and uncertain legacy. William Joyce was on the air most nights for fifteen or more minutes, for over five years. The quotes above are perfectly typical of the type of material he presented, so his output of calumny and detraction was vast. If you measure his importance by the number of people who knew his works, and by the number of people who talked about him, you might say he was the most important figure (in Britain) in the War. But as to his real influence, it is hard to judge.

We know that a large number of persons laughed at him, and many said they did not take him seriously. Yet the vitriol poured on him during the War suggests that he was hitting some nerves somewhere, and it could be that his constant preaching of uncertainty did have some effect on the less staunch.

But, in any case, by January 3rd, 1946, when he was executed, it seemed that he was almost a forgotten figure, so small was the ripple caused by his execution. Here in Australia, the *SMH* gave his death only five column-inches on Page One.

RATIONING IS HERE TO STAY

At the end of the War, every man, woman and child **was the proud owner of one or two or more ration book**s. In each of these was a number of coupons, issued by a caring Federal government, that allowed the purchase of some commodity such as butter or petrol. Of course, people still had to pay out their cash but, without these coupons, no sale was possible. So that every six months or so, new coupons were issued to all, and with due regard to the use-by dates on these, articles could be exchanged for clearly defined quantities of specific goods.

To keep the populace up to date, little notices were placed everywhere telling you what coupons you could currently use. For example, this month you could use the **black** meat coupons 64 to 70 until March 19. After that, the **red** meat coupons, current till April 25, were to be used. On the same notices, the rules for tea and sugar were recorded. After the expiry date, the coupons were useless.

For clothing, **the expiry dates were measured in years** to allow for the longer life of articles. For petrol, three months was allowed, so that you could save them up and take a binge trip of about 100 miles if you were lucky. The notices were in shops and newspapers and Post Offices so there was no use coming in with a handful of expired coupons and saying you hadn't been told. The Canberra men had good reasons to impose this system. In simple terms, there were not enough goods and services to go round.

So, to preserve the rich and powerful from the gluttony they supposedly wanted, equal rations were handed to all. And of course, the quotas thus allocated were of a smallish size, so that national consumption was thereby reduced. And it was comprehensive. It applied to most commodities that you can think of. And **if it was not rationed, then it was in short supply**, which meant ordering and then waiting for weeks; or there were simply none to be bought. For example, how many pushbikes were put in the rack because there were **no** rubber tyres for replacements?

There was no doubt that it was a real pain in the neck. For every person in the nation, it meant real austerity. If you wanted a cup of tea, or sugar in your tea, or a jelly lamington, or a saveloy, then you had to think carefully. If you wanted a new Geordie cap, or a balaclava, or a pair of rubber sandshoes, you most likely missed out. If you had a car, and it had tyres that were still useable, then you had only enough petrol to get you there – but not back. Rationing nagged away all day, every day, ever present, everywhere. So everyone grizzled all the time. No one in those days talked about sex, or religion or politics. But they did talk about rationing, and how it was excessive, and unnecessary, and useless; about how it was going to be abolished, or more likely, increased two fold; about thriving blackmarkets whereby the rich lived in gross opulence; about American servicemen who each had four pork chops and a bottle of whisky three times a day, and who slept under dozens of woollen blankets.

Yet the remarkable thing is that there was no real opposition to rationing. Just lots of grumbling. **If** the nation as a whole **had thought that this War was not worth fighting**, then this system would have failed. **If** there had been doubts about the justice of the War, or if there had been anything less than wholesale commitment, then the administrative efforts of the Canberra bureaucrats would have failed against the concerted resentment built up. **But it did succeed**. Consumption was cut back. For the duration of the War, all manner of privations were foisted onto the population. And they accepted it. Of course, at the time, they thought it was just for the duration of the War, and that peace and steak and eggs would all return at the same time. **This did not happen,** as we shall see.

NEWS AND VIEWS

For the next two pages, I will give you a few Letters that show some of the issues that faced people in this post-war world. In most cases, **we will come back later and explore them more.**

Some rehab problems.   Here is a letter from a tailor who went into the services. His premises were requisitioned by the military, but now he can't get them back.

Letters. What efforts are being made by Rehabilitation on behalf of ex-servicemen in a similar situation to myself, men who prior to the war ran their own business and who now suffer the handicap of having no premises.?

With the reported reduction of Federal Departments, space must become available. I have attempted to work at home, but one cannot persuade hands to travel out to the suburbs, nor is there any convenience in a private house to establish a workroom. Also, in the tailoring trade, one must be in a spot convenient to customers.

Amongst others, my name has been on agents' lists for months, once getting near to occupancy, only to find at the last minute that another government department had taken over for a long period.

What can I do? I should have stayed at home, and kept my premises and business.

Home owners' losses. The Government in 1941 brought down measures that froze the rent on properties. This meant that **the renter will continue to pay rent at the 1941 level** until the Government decides otherwise. Given that inflation then was as relentless as it is now, this news was welcomed by renters, but was **a disaster for landlords**.

Letters. For some years now many retired men and women, depending on their savings for their livelihood, have found it impossible to derive any benefit from the increased value of their property, in which they have invested their savings.

The majority of tenants are receiving higher wages. The house owners are too old to seek work afresh. Why, therefore, should they not be allowed the same increase in their rental income?

For any necessary repairs to their properties, they have to pay exorbitant charges, and their income tax is at a much higher rate than the worker's. Frail men and women should not be legislated out of their just rights.

Comment. The rent being lost by landlords was bad enough in 1946. But the situation continued until around 1966.

Britain's food supply. I make the point later in this book that 1946 should be known **in Europe as the Year of Hunger and Famine**. Here is an early look at the situation in Britain.

Letters. Any shop that has food has a long queue outside, of perhaps 50 yards. Seeing dozens of these queues is a most depressing sight when you realise that the food will probably be sold out before the end of the queue reaches the counter.

It was almost impossible to get a meal in cafes, and I have often walked the streets hungry. Nowhere in Britain did I hear it suggested that they reduce their own rations to send it to Europe. What concerns them is that when the war ended they expected more food, but in fact their rations now are lower than in the war.

When I returned from my prison camp to Australia, I was astounded to see how much food we have. I had not thought it possible that we could have so much, while the British have so little. We must remedy this position. Surely our memories are not so short that we are forgetting already what the British people stood up to during the war.

FEBRUARY NEWS ITEMS

Britain, America and Australia agreed that **Australia should contribute several thousand servicemen** and three ships **to the occupation of Japan** for an unspecified period. Their duties will include maintaining law and order, and supervising the disarmament process....

This marked the beginning of a period in which our soldiers started to **fraternise with Japanese girls**, and led to all sorts of problems, and solutions, over **Japanese war brides and their entry into White Australia.**

Four thousand brides and infants of US servicemen will leave Sydney for the US in the next four months. The first two batches, of 800 each, will leave on the *Mariposa* and *Monterey* next week.

Milk rationing, that had been in place for years round Australia, **was removed in NSW** in the first week of February. Immediately **the consumption increased dramatically**, and the Milk Board was forced to **re-introduce rationing**. This was to allow time for the Board to arrange new distribution channels.

Soldiers were to be repatriated back to Australia on a points system. Those with longer service got more points, and so too did those who were judged to be necessary for more important industries such as agriculture. Every soldier by now knew how many points he had....

When a troopship, the *Georgetown Victory*, berthed in Rabaul, sections of it were taken over by it **troops anxious to get home**. They were told to get off and make way for **those troops who had a greater number of points**. They refused, and left the ship only after **the crew had battened**

down the hatches, locked the doors, and cut off the water supply.

Short-term strikes were part of everyday life. For example, on February 21st, the front page of the Sydney Morning Herald (SMH) carried stories of strikes by shunters, railwaymen, milkos, miners, and bakers. This was just a normal day....

But it was **much worse overseas**. On the same day, Indian sailors mutinied and took over 24 of the 28 British ships in Bombay. Police and troops used machine guns to fire on rioters in Cairo. The new United Nations were already snarling at each other over disputes involving Greece and Java. **The world was unsettled**, it was in the grip of planet-wide hunger, and hundreds of groups and nations were planning disruptions of all sorts to finally **remove the last vestiges of colonial rule....**

Strikes in Australia, granted very annoying, should be seen from this perspective.

Officials at the **GI** Brides Transport Office in London report that many **returned GIs are not seeking to bring their brides back home to America**. "While they were in England, they dreamed rosy dreams. Army pay was high and they boasted about the good times they would have back home"....

"But back there, **they find that jobs are hard to get, and life is difficult**. They lose heart, and think **the best way out is divorce**." The brides are still officially British. Divorce is looming for quite a few.

THE UNITED NATIONS

On New Year's Day, politicians from around the world started milling round in London. One of the reasons for hope in the future was the formation of a new group, the United Nations, that was to open a few days later. People and politicians were cautious in welcoming it. They had seen that its parent, the League of Nations, had been of limited value between the two Wars. Indeed, it has often been said that the fact that the Second World War did break out shows that the League was a complete failure. Still, men of good sense argued that there was a need for an international group empowered to get involved in world policy, and saw it – having learned lessons from the League – as the potential solution to many problems.

Official statements indicate some genuine enthusiasm at the top level, liberally dosed with realistic pompous caution. For example, His Majesty King George VI, speaking at a banquet to welcome the 51 delegates to the first meeting of the United Nations, said:

> The people of the British Commonwealth and Empire who, although hard beset, did not fail mankind in its hour of deadliest peril, will not fail it now in the task of laying the foundations of a new world. The high task is to build a world where such a conflict as lately brought us all to the verge of annihilation must never be repeated.

Again, the British Prime Minister, Clement Attlee, welcomed delegates to the inaugural meeting of the General Assembly of the United Nations, on January 7, in the Central Hall in Westminster. He told the delegates that:

> We realise that, as never before, a choice is offered to mankind. Should there be a Third World War, the long upward progress of civilisation may be halted

for generations, and the work of centuries brought to nought. We, the British Commonwealth and Empire, will whole-heartedly stand behind the UNO, at which, for the second time in 27 years, mankind will attempt to secure world peace. The ultimate aim is not just to secure world peace, but the creation of a world of security and freedom governed by justice and the moral law.

Comment. Of course, such wonderful rhetoric was not always matched by wonderful actions. Attlee knew full well that, even as he spoke, the leading nations were setting up the UN so that only the most powerful nations would hold the reins of power. **Over the years**, many disputes and treaties have since been settled in ways that completely deny the UN Charter. And some of its fiascos are unforgettable. Does anyone remember Bob Menzies, under UN auspices, attempting to solve the 1956 Suez crisis? What about Nikita Kruschev when he took his shoe off and belted the rostrum as he addressed the General Assembly? And do not forget Colin Powell, then US Secretary of State. He showed satellite photos of chook sheds in Oodnadatta and apparently convinced the General Assembly that they represented factories in Iraq that were intent on making Weapons of Mass Destruction.

Yet, the UN's almost-forgotten role in refugee work has been extensive. Ditto for its efforts through the World Health Organisation. Then, to be critical again, its World Bank – acting as an agent of US foreign policy in undeveloped countries – has left an at-times sorry legacy.

THE UN IN PRACTICE

After the initial excitement of creating a new forum for world peace, the UN settled down in February to the humdrum of working out how it would achieve that peace. The one thing that was dominant in the minds of the big powers was that they should always have as much power as they could get.

So, their Charter set up a system that said the four major nations of the time should each have a power of veto over any decision that the other nations should make. No matter what the rights and wrongs were of a situation, one Great Power, say Russia, could veto any decision made, and forestall any action.

Australia's Doc Evatt argued at length against this system. He wanted a more democratic form of governance, where every nation, big or small, had equal rights on any decision. Of course, **this was just a waste of breath**. The veto system has survived to this day, and the other Big Powers, Britain, the US and France, have all used it as well as the Russian, whenever world opinion went against them.

Now, 70 years later, despite this, the UN still exists, and unlike the League of Nations before it, it is often a force for peace, and sometimes a voice for moderation. It might not be perfect – it is a long way from that – but it seems to me that the world would be a more perilous place if it was to fade away.

FOOD SHORTAGES

On the world stage, in European countries that had been devastated by bombings and invasions, real hunger and shortages of all commodities struck the masses, often homeless, with devastating force. All the lines of supply, that the various military forces had been keeping open, had now collapsed, and **famine and starvation were serious possibilities for tens of millions.**

Germany, the biggest loser in the War, was by now in the depths of its despair. After the War, it had been divided into four sectors. Britain, France, and the USA each took their share. And of course, the new arch-villain, Russia, carved out its own sphere of influence. Within the British sector, early in 1946, the avalanche arrived, and the following sample of official press releases tells something of the story. Note that the average food intake for an Australian adult is measured at **above 2,500 calories per day.**

Hamburg. From next Monday, rations for 20 million German civilians in the British zone will be cut by one third, and the people have been warned that further cuts may be necessary. They are now getting 1,500 calories a day. This is to be cut to 1014 calories. **The British Government has accepted as inevitable** the existence of widespread starvation in Germany. It expects that hundreds of thousands of deaths will result.

Sheffield. The gravest statement yet made by the Minister, Mr John Hind, on the impending starvation in Central Europe. He said, in a speech at Sheffield, "It is a matter of days whether or not 23 million people are going to starve in the streets. Unless 150,000 tons of wheat arrive in Germany before the end of the month, the daily rations of the people will not be 1,000 calories but 700 or even 500."

Hamburg. Food rioting has broken out in Hamburg, where the German population has eaten seven-eighths of their monthly ration in a fortnight. In spite of special precautions taken against the raiding of food shops, at least 10 cases of looting were reported today.

Hamburg. Looting of food trains has become widespread in the Rhur Valley, and lawlessness has reached new heights. In one incident, 35 of them were arrested, but 28 of them were freed by mobs who attacked the police. In another incident, a mob of about 1,000 stopped a food train. British military police arrested 70 of them, and they will appear in a military court. Loudspeaker vans are touring the countryside warning that crowds will be dispersed by force.

In Britain, meanwhile, the scarcity of food and all goods was of course much more severe than in Australia, because the Brits had experienced en masse the wartime ravages that we here had only sampled. Their plight can perhaps be summarised and illustrated by the following news item. It appeared in a local newspaper, under the heading *"Bananas now come straight to you."*

February, 1946: A most remarkable event occurred here today. A happening that signalled that the War was over, that peace was truly upon us, and that happy days will soon be here again. In a year crowded with occasions to remember, this was indeed the most memorable. **After a gap of seven years, Britain received its first post-war shipment of bananas.**

Here we have at last real proof that the war is over. The bombers might have gone away, London might have stopped burning. Our gas masks are in the attic. But, up till now, there was always doubt whether the war would somehow come back again. But here is definite proof. **Bananas are back; therefore the War is over.**

For the benefit of children to whom the banana was some delectable curiosity, an exotic fruit that their elders had told them about, but they had never eaten, the Daily Express published a picture of one, and its kitchen column told how to cook it.

Bananas were the first luxury cargo to be sacrificed to the needs of war, and the arrival of the gaily be-flagged Tilapa brought all work at Avonmouth docks to a halt.

Spectators gave vent to their excitement in rounds of cheering, and there was a scramble for a ripe banana which was thrown on to the dock and awarded to a 10-year-old daughter of a dock worker.

Unloading today was made a civic occasion, with the Lord Mayor of Bristol and members of the dock committee in attendance. Town bands made lots of noise, every one of them playing a different tune at the same time. It was truly a gala occasion in the best British tradition.

Back in Australia, a snapshot of one little problem highlights official attitudes towards rationing. It concerns rice. In Australia in 1946, rice was not an essential commodity. The number of Asians in this country was very small, in fact miniscule, due to fanatical enforcement of the White Australia Policy. And none of their cultural cuisine had crossed the Pacific to these shores. So curried prawns and rice was truly an exotic dish, and rice generally was rarely on the menu of the average household. Still, Mums nationwide did like to dabble now and then, and **baked rice turned up** say once a fortnight to make a bit of a change. So there was a distinct absence of glee when the following news item was released.

British Ministry of Food. The Ministry has accepted Australia's offer of 20,000 tons of dressed rice from the 1946-47 crop. The Australian Minister for Commerce and Agriculture, Mr Scully, said it meant **no rice would be available in Australia from the next harvest,** except for invalids, hospitals, and rice-eating aliens.

Mr. Scully said that the British Food Ministry had indicated that, in accordance with the short-haul policy to economise on use of shipping, **the rice would not go to Britain itself**. The Ministry would ensure, however, that it went to British territories.

A few weeks later, Mr. Vincent, a Senior Inspector with NSW Agriculture, was able to happily announce that "the promise of substantial rice crops in Australia is much better than it was several months ago. With reasonable weather, the crop should be extremely good. I have never seen it looking better at this time of year, and the flag is particularly green. But no matter how high this season's yield might be, **the Australian public will get none**. It is pleasing to think there will be more for export to those whose lives depend on it".

This artificial shortage of rice was maintained in various forms until the early 1950's.

Three letters from ex-servicemen shed more light on our position in a world context.

Letters, M Harrison. I wish to record a few of my first impressions of Australia after five years' overseas RAAF service.

First and foremost, the apathy and complacency of many of the people have struck me most forcibly, and it is to these people that I address my remarks. In the British Isles where total war has been brought home very visibly to the people in the past years, where the country has been scarred, and homes bombed out, seldom does one hear of complaints from the people. But here in Australia, where none of these conditions exist, one finds people complaining when they have no reason to do so.

One thing that makes returning servicemen see red is to hear people (who have never suffered a food shortage) complaining about being unable to get sufficient of this or that, while there are others in the world who have not had these things for years.

We can surely have no complaints to air as compared with our British cousins. So **wake up** Australia and let us hear less complaining.

Letters, L Frost. Now that the world at last realises the food positioning in Europe and especially in Britain, it is time for this country to **wake up** to these facts. That we in Australia could feed the whole of Europe with the food product from our arable land.

As an army cook, I have more than an idea about what really is wanted. In three months that I have spent in Brisbane, I have seen several tons of bread, and about a ton of meat and vegetables, many 14 lb tins of dehydrated vegetables, flour, oatmeal, vegetables, fresh meat, about a ton of dried fruit, and numerous other items of **food burned or dumped**.

In civilian life, I was a dairy farmer. In my present position, I am a burden on the taxpayers of Australia like thousands more in uniform. Why can we not do something that will make Australia tops – something to aid Australia and at the same time, aid thousands of starving families, mine among them. Many farms have closed during the war because of labour shortages, and they are still closing down because men of experience are still in the Forces as key men.

Letters, R Donald. I noticed in your paper on Friday a picture of the Japanese steamer Daikai Maru, and read that the crew were loading butter for the voyage home.

I, as an ex-POW of the Eighth Division, worked on the Thailand Burma railway under horrible conditions and starvation, and got just enough rice to exist on. I lost quite a few of my pals through starvation. People in England are starving. We are willing to **make sacrifices for our Mother Country, but not for the Japanese.**

Comment. The above writers were correct of course in saying that Australia was well off compared to other places. And to say that we complained a lot is also true. But, that did not mean we were a heartless bloated lot who did not care.

As we will see later, when it came to supporting England (and not Japan) we were very generous indeed. This was at the official level, and also true for the individual.

Be that as it may, however, one of the wonders of wartime Australia was that we did complain a lot about shortages. **But that is where the negativity stopped.** As a nation, we had a good healthy whinge, as good British stock should, then got on with our business.

NEWS AND VIEWS

Golf. Norman von Nida was a famous Australian golfer. He was short in stature and very short of temper. As evidenced here, after a confrontation with a cine-cameraman.

..... The camera-man said nothing, but a spectator butted in with "Go on, you are a bad sport. All you Australians are the same. You are accusing the crowd of putting you off your shot."

I got angry. "Why can't you keep your big mouth shut. If you don't, I will shut it for you." He said "Oh you will, huh? When? "

I got really angry then and said "right now if you like." I then told him I would see him later, and went on to the next tee." I went back later after finishing the round, but there was no sign of him.

Sydney Radio Station 2UW, and **radio** Stations in all cities, was heavily advertising a World Heavyweight Title fight between two boxers. **You could listen to it in your own living room for no charge, they said. WOW!**

A fight between Australians Vic Patrick and the challenger Tommy Burns was also filling the papers with similar ads. As it turned out, this latter fight was one of the great fights of the decade.

That, however, is not my point here. Rather, I want to remind you **that boxing was one of the sports that millions of people followed daily**, just as much as they follow Rugby League and Australian Rules today. It did not matter whether fights were in the USA or in Australia, a fan could tell you who had fought whom, and who today's and yesterday's champions were, and whether contenders now were currently a couple of ounces over-weight.

Comment. Pre-war, for the masses of uneducated, **boxing was seen as one of the very few ways out of poverty**. With the new vistas opening up in the post-war years, it would **eventually** became apparent that there were better ways to climb the economic ladder than **getting your brains bashed out** at regular intervals. But that was not yet obvious to the strugglers, and so boxing was still a very popular sport.

As a matter of interest, all the boxing broadcasts on this Station were sponsored by Gillette Razors. Boxing, they said, was a cut-throat business.

Cricket. Bill O'Rielly, Ern Toshack, Sid Barnes and Ray Lindwall had a problem in early 1946. They were selected to play cricket for NSW and for Australia, and were each awarded two blazers to wear to official occasions. The trouble was that a **blazer cost nine clothing coupon**s, for a total of 18 coupons. This would have used up most of their annual allowance. And borrowing coupons from friends and family was quite illegal. Somehow though, they did get their blazers, and avoided the long arm of Federal law.

MARCH NEWS ITEMS

Good news – for some. **The sugar ration will be increased** from one pound per month to two pounds. This is for NSW, Victoria, Tasmania and Western Australia. **More good news – for some. Ten new air-conditioned trains will be introduced to NSW country services**. On the Sydney to Newcastle run of 100 miles. The rest of the State (the hot part) can sweat it out.

General Thomas Blamey, along with many senior military men, **had recently retired**. So now he was free to criticise the Government. He did so with a broadside that complained about the rule that said that **top military men in Australia could not be awarded King's Honours....**

He pointed out that, in the British Army, generals were prominent in the King's lists. "Why do our politicians continue to pull the top military down? Have they committed some criminal offence in becoming your leaders?" This was another sign of the **war-long discomfort that existed between our military and our politicians**.

Prime Minister Chifley said tonight that he will authorise a big campaign against **black marketing in meat**. He said that when individuals bought above-ration meat, they decreased the **amount that can be sent to hungry Britain**. He hoped to send a record 300,000 tons of meat this year, and black market trading would stop this.

Things are getting really serious in NSW.Tooths Brewery produces 70 per cent on the State's beer, and now it has been **closed by a really threatening strike**.

A report from London says that jitterbugging and swing are being deserted for a revival of the "naughty nineties" dances. The American crazes are being replaced by **the polka, the lancers, quadrilles, schottisches, and waltzes**. Dancers of **all ages** are joining "Gay Nineties" clubs, whereas the American forms are mainly for **adolescents**.

The US Army is refusing permission for its Occupation soldiers to marry German girls, even those that are pregnant. No peace treaty has been signed between the two nations, and **they are officially still at war.** "We as a nation should not confer **the benefits** which come to the wife of a US soldier **upon an enemy of the US**."

Norman Gilroy was elected to the Vatican's Sacred College of **Cardinals** on February 18th. He was the **first Australian Catholic to receive that honou**r. He returned to his Sydney archdiocese about a month later. He received "a hero's welcome from great crowds."

Squatting in unusued premises is starting to become a city problem. **In London**, many buildings, that were condemned after the bombings, are now being occupied by homeless persons. This is against the law, but there are so many homeless that **it is hard to police**....

In Australia, where homelessness is nowhere near so severe a problem, it is nevertheless becoming too common **as returned diggers seek rooms for their families**.

The Labor Minister for Immigration, **Arthur Calwell,has refused visas for four famous Australian tennis players to go to Wimbledon this year**. He cited the long waiting-list for war brides for berths. Critics of Calwell pointed out that the **players would have flown, and that the brides always came by ship**. The Minister, in his wisdom, remained unmoved.

GORDON BENNETT'S ESCAPE

James Gordon Bennett was born in 1887. He served with distinction in WWI, and accumulated several awards, including the Distinguished Service Order. After the war, he went back to his commercial interests, but remained an obsessed member of the Civilian Military Forces. This was a part-time army, that exercised a couple of nights a week, with the odd weekend or annual camp.

The **permanent** Army Officers regarded the CMF as a joke, and the CMF in return thought of the permanents as White Hall Warriors who stuck with obsolete attitudes to warfare. By the time that WWII was forced upon us, Bennett had made many enemies among the officers of the regulars, and that would come back to visit him in later days.

When Australia was sending its troops to Singapore in 1941, Bennett was appointed to the Eighth Division as their commander. Later in that year, when the Japanese invaded Malaya and then moved down to the island of Singapore, Australian losses were heavy. In the long run, by the middle of February, 1,789 Australians were killed, and 1,306 were wounded. The living were forced to lay down their arms, and became prisoners-of-war. **What a tragedy**.

There were 15,000 such prisoners, and they were marched away to places like Changi and Burma. But that brings us back to Bennett. As news of the **fall of Singapore** gradually became known over the next three years**, half the population of Australia came to believe that that number should have been 15,001.**

BENNETT BACK IN AUSTRALIA

Bennett and his officers arranged a cease-fire with the Japanese. Bennett immediately handed over command of the forces to a brigadier, and left, with Australia as his destination. After a nerve wracking journey, he arrived back in Australia on March 1st, 1942. His welcome from the War Cabinet members in Canberra was cordial but restrained, and reflected the fact that many people, army officials and civilians, were bewildered by his presence here. After all, they thought, should he not be with his troops?

The Prime Minister did approve a release to the Press that included the statement that "his leadership and conduct were in complete conformity with his duty to the men under his command and to his country."

That did not settle the matter. Chifley and Deputy PM Forde might have been satisfied, but there were many who were not. They considered that **the duty of a defeated leader was to stay with his troops** and to do what he could to make sure they got reasonable treatment. If 15,000 soldiers were to be locked up, for years as it turned out, why should their leader escape? **Had he in fact deserted?** Had he earned the white feathers that were sent to him?

There were lots of people who said he had been justified in leaving. Apart from technical arguments that emerged from later hearings into the matter, there were the immediately obvious. He had gained knowledge of Japanese jungle tactics that he thought would be most useful for subsequent troops. He felt he had a duty, as a prisoner-of-war, to escape, and thus be able to return to the fray. He said that there was no need for him to fend for the prisoners, because he had left behind a host of other officers who were well able to do that.

His opponents saw things differently. Not surprisingly, these **opponents were headed by the permanent Army officers, the Staff officers, the ones he had been persistently alienating for year**s. Most of these thought that he should not have left his troops. Some said he was driven by personal ambition, that he considered himself absolutely and uniquely indispensable to the nation's war making. Others said that he came back because he hoped to get promoted to the new post of Commander-in-Chief. Military purists insisted that he had received no instruction to leave, and from the military's point of view, he was not justified in doing so.

But this country was at the time engaged in a full-time war. This was not the time to encourage a wide national debate on matters such as desertion by high-ranking officers. So for almost three years, the matter was put on the back-burner. Bennett was given a command in Western Australia, well away from the limelight. It became obvious that he was there permanently, and that he was a person not acceptable.

PERCIVAL STIRS THE POT

In mid 1945, the English General, Percival, who had exercised overall command of all troops in Malaya and Singapore, was released from Changi after the war. He then reported that "I have to report that Bennett, voluntarily and without permission, relinquished the command of the AIF, on February 15, 1942, on which the capitulation of the British Forces in Malaya took place." At the same time, a couple of other reports from different officers emerged from the recesses of the Staff Office, and these too were highly critical of Bennett's departure from Singapore. The matter now open for consideration was that he had apparently issued orders that

none of his officers should escape, yet he took advantage of his own position to escape himself.

Now, the Army is a funny animal. It has its own sets of values and precedents, and its own rules and laws. These run parallel to the laws of the land, and often coincide with them. But it reserves the right to run its own courts and its own systems when it thinks it proper. In wartime, the army of course has great power in society, and whatever it does will always attract a great deal of external scrutiny. So when General Blamey issued orders on October 10, 1945, for a military court of enquiry into the matter, it caused a sensation.

The court opened on the 26th of October, and sat till the 30th. It heard evidence from nine officers who had been on Bennett's staff, and most of these had just been released from Changi and recently repatriated. The evidence was muddied by the fact that so much time had elapsed since the events occurred, and the fact that the witnesses had not been able to retain any of the written notes they had all taken prior to their imprisonment. But **the military court came to the decision that Bennett was not justified in handing over his command and leaving Singapore.**

Blamey took this report, and passed it on to the Government, who decided, in view of the public interest that this private enquiry had provoked, to **hold a Royal Commission**. It began its sittings on November 26th, and sat till December 13th. Much of its evidence was the same as that given earlier, with a few more witnesses included.

The Commission, late in February 1946, gave its opinion in measured, diplomatic terms. It pointed out that Bennett had not been justified in leaving his post, but that he had **simply been guilty of an error of judgement**. It went on to say that he had acted from the best of intentions, and with the interests of Australia at heart.

By this time, though, the war was well and truly over, so now it could all be told. The time was now rife for a full-scale argument about the so-called desertion, and the various media erupted in March with a **myriad of opinions**.

For example, a new one was that when McArthur left **his** troops in the Philippines, he had been ordered to do so. And when Blamey left **his** troops in Greece, he too had been ordered to do so. But Bennett had not been so ordered; he had just left. Surely this was desertion.

To Bennett's supporters, this man was a gallant soldier who had risked his life to return to Australia so that he could bring valuable information about the right way to fight the enemy in the jungle. He was not a deserter, he was a hero.

Other commentators were subsequently not so generous. Many referred to the fact that Bennet was very ambitious, and chose to escape in order to further his own ends. Writer after writer claimed that he had often spoken of aspirations of becoming Commander-in-Chief of Australia's forces, and the idea that this position was soon to be filled spurred him on.

In the long run, no clear cut decision was possible. **Supporters and detractors clung tenaciously to their respective views.** The Royal Commission, though helpful, did not resolve the issue at all. But in any case, the matter remained unsettled then; and, even now, the question of whether or not he deserted, in the true sense of the word, remains unanswered.

CLOTHING RATIONS

The rationing of clothing by coupons was introduced in June 1942. It applied to almost any clothing then worn, as well as to all headwear types, footwear, and wool for knitting. And, as a separate measure, sheets and blankets, pillow cases and all cotton goods. The aim of the scheme was to reduce consumption by about half, so that you could guarantee that no matter what scheme the Government could devise, everyone had some complaint or other followed by more complaints.

Some of the items included on the list of articles that could be bought included a number that **are not at all fashionable now**. For example, corsets are **now** rarely heard of, and are restricted mainly to older people who have lived their lives with them, and those with worrying medical conditions. **Bloomers, woven**, are probably rarer, and **petticoats and knitted vests** are also currently on the outer. **Woollen overcoats** have been almost relegated to the dustbin, despite all their cosy warmth – perhaps it was their capacity to soak up water that decided their fate. And finally, **woollen dresses and skirts** are still available in more expensive shops, but not the old clunkers of yesteryear. Note that there was no mention of nylons or synthetics. These came only after the War – does anyone remember Alec Guiness in *The Man in the White Suit?*

Notable now for their absence were **womens' pants** of any description. Women had become aware of slacks in the War, as the common dress in factories. They are **not** included in the Coupon Table because at that time **they were issued** to women by the Government, and were considered to be work related, and not for private consumption. So of course, **jeans** were not there either. Nor **bikinis.** Nor **mini skirts**. But for men, there were some chic **underpants – long knitted** as well as those indispensable **woven singlets.**

The data on garment life in years shows some extremes, at least by today's standards. It is hard to imagine any active surfer keeping a bathing suit for ten years, or that a pair of shoes could be made to last for two years of constant wear. Woollen overcoats were supposed to last, and eight years was deemed a useful life. Though the longevity award went to **dressing gowns (men and women), which had a service life of twenty years.**

For years, until about 1950 when the last of these regulations were repealed, wardrobes gradually got older and shabbier. Even the British war brides on arrival here described our women folk as dowdy – and that coming from such fashion centres as Birmingham and North Scotland.

One great worry was a shortage of suits, **for all men**, though ex-servicemen got all the publicity. These ex-Diggers were released into civilian life with only their uniforms, and theoretically a suit and other basic essentials. They had no stock of older clothes to fall back on. But worse, there were problems in getting the suits. On May 6, a clothing industry spokesman said that:

As they are discharged in their thousands, men and women from the services are overwhelming the tailors with orders for new civilian outfits, but the lack of materials leaves the supply far behind the demand. Many civilians, who for years have been wearing their suits threadbare are also in an embarrassing plight. They have contented themselves with the thought that as soon as the temporary demand of the returned servicemen was satisfied, there would be at least enough good Australian woolen cloth for everyone. But the picture is steadily becoming worse. For civilian and soldier alike, the new suit is becoming a will-o'-the-wisp.

The problem really stemmed from the fact that Australia, rich in raw wool, sent this commodity to Britain for initial processing; and then imported it back to here. It came in either as finished goods, or it was then processed further in local factories. The same end result was true for cotton, with Manchester cotton the epitome of excellence. So with Britain not exporting much at all, there was the inevitable shortage of material. This was compounded by other factors. Mr Robinson Brown, President of the Master Tailors' Association of NSW, elucidates.

Letters. The principal cause is the shortage of girl labour in textile factories, but the position has been aggravated by the restrictions on the use of power, which stopped all production for several weeks. There are also shortages of men's hats and boots and shoes, but the position is not as serious as in the case of suits and shirts.

The labour position has been getting steadily worse for the last two or three years. In the four principal wool-cloth mills in NSW, the female labour has declined by 40 per cent in the last two years despite the fact that factory conditions and amenities are highly spoken of by everyone who has seen them. Wages are good, and it is stated that girls entering the industry are assured of permanent work for all their working lives. But, as an official pointed out yesterday, it is useless to find more labour for suit and shirt manufacture, when the raw materials are practically unprocurable.

"**Clothing Observed**" came up with another reason.

Letters. While we are receiving little or no material from Britain, **we are exporting a substantial portion of our own output**. To seek valuable export markets may be sound policy, but as Mr.Abbott protested a few days ago, Australia is sending woollen goods to markets where she can never hope to compete. He spoke of the fantastic desire to export wool here, there, and everywhere. A better balance should be struck between home and export needs, so that the ex-soldier is not penalised for the sake of sales which have no value in terms of future trade.

Apart from the men, **women had their own problems**. At a meeting of the Housewives Association in Sydney on March 6th, the president, Mrs Glencross removed her shoe, held it up to the meeting, and announced it as pre-war. She was refuting statements by some members that much of the good-value clothing seen today was from the black market.

"Like practically all my clothes, these shoes I am wearing were bought before the war," she said. The guest speaker, Mrs Evelyn Gardiner, supported Mrs Glencross. "Everything I stand up in is at least six years old. My hat is a renovation, my dress is made from a pair of my husband's trousers and lined with an old evening frock, my lisle stockings and my underwear were bought in London seven years ago, and my shoes were also brought from London. And as an actress, I am expected to dress."

For the ladies, though, there was the promise of a new wonder fabric, nylon:

Advertorial, Mar 7: There is magic in the word "nylon" for women, who are as ready to riot in Australia as they are in America if nylon stockings, let alone printed fabrics, are ever advertised. During the war, nylon went into parachutes, but now it is returning to civilian use not only in stockings, but in dress fabrics. The first opportunity women will have to see nylon fabrics will be at an exhibition of Ascher fabrics designed by famous English and Continental artists which are being brought here by Miss Matilda Etches.

The exhibition will include 61 lengths and 127 scarf-squares of Ascher fabrics as well as printed nylon designed by Christian Berard, a French theatre and fashion artist. Miss Etches is expected in Sydney on March 11.

At a private view of the Ascher fabrics at the Australia Hotel on March 19, Mr. Max Lawson will auction some lengths – including nylon which is being flown here specially – for the Red Cross for Britain Fund. The fabrics will be on view at the New Studio, 25 Rowe Street, for about a week in March.

Then again, technology was ever-ready to spring to the rescue:

Advertorial, Mar 20. It is no exaggeration to say that many girls have become so used to the pleasure of **going bare-legged during the war** that it will take the VERY dreamiest pure silk or rare nylon to lure them back into the confines of stockings. Indeed, now that CYCLAX **stockingless cream** has made its welcome return to our midst, it is doubtful if even those charms will lure us, because the Cyclax cream **IS** as sheerly lovely in appearance as the finest stockings ever will be. And it's certainly much freer to wear. The shades are exquisite, rose, beige, honey beige and romany beige. And how smoothly it stays on.

Note that, for larger children, the Government was all compassion. Children who were bigger than normal for their ages will be issued again this year with extra ration coupons. For example, boys born after May 1930, who are eight stone or more, will be given 25 coupons. Schools will apply for and distribute the issue to children attending schools. Others will need to fill in Form Rg 21, and send it to the Director General. The child's ration book must also be sent in.

HAND-ME-DOWNS WERE STILL IN VOGUE

Every family in the nation had quickly realised that old clothing would have to be kept in circulation for a long time. This meant that when the oldest boy grew out of a jumper, there was no shopping spree to buy a new one. Rather, the old jumper was handed down to the next boy in line, and Mum had to knit a new one for the older boy. But where could she get the wool?

The only place was from old jumpers that someone else had discarded. So she unpulled that wool, rolled it into balls, got out the size 12 knitting needles, and purled away. If she ran out of a particular colour, she had to blend in a different colour and size of wool from another jumper. It all added to the variety of life. I know for a fact that some boys refused to wear the end product, but they gave in when winter hit.

THE END OF CLOTHES RATIONING?

At one time in March, people got all excited because the Army Disposal Stores were now selling tons and tons of ex-army boots, shirts, trousers and the like. There were a few suggestions that because they had already been made, and that they were surplus to normal expectations, they could be sold without coupons. Alas, though, that was not to be, and so coupons were still needed for these alluring items.

Then, once a month, some Government Minister would win a small amount of temporary public favour by saying that he expected clothing would soon be removed from rationing. Of course, this was all rubbish, and there was no change for years. So, at the end of 1946, new ration books were issued. Clothes rationing was here to stay for a long time.

A GREAT NEW DEVICE

Advertorial. This week we have been talking to the **Floor Sanding people**. And we have been sold on the idea of having all our floors done over by the sanding and polishing process. It's so modern, that lovely, sleek, smooth, gleaming stretch of stained or natural wood. They send their experts out to anywhere near the city, and they will look at your floors. No matter how dreadful they might appear to you now, they'll show you samples of how that particular wood will look, polished in natural grain, or stained to the shade of your choice. **The drabbest old floor can be worked up to an interior decorator's dream.** And the cost is less than a quarter the cost of carpets. Just needs a mop-over, and **silverfish can't eat it. Ring MA8358.**

Comment. This of course was not just the old-fashioned three-wheel floor polisher. The product advertised here was **a floor sander**. The marketing of this to the plebs was new at the time. Note **the phone numbers for Sydney**. Just two letters, and four digits.

Keeping Britain clean. The Australian government said that it was prepared to make 5,000 tons of soap available to Britain for purchase. It was now learned that Britain had accepted the offer. This will be the first time that Britain, which before the War was a big soap exporter, has imported soap from Australia. **Remember the jokes about the great unwashed Brits, and their weekly baths?**

Wow. What a relief. The Surgeon-General's Office of the US Army has announced that tests conducted on male guinea pigs showed that **men who feared baldness and sterility from radar waves have no further cause for worry.**

APRIL NEWS ITEMS

Good news for the entire world. America now has a **stockpile of 1,500 atom bombs**, and is producing more "at a great rate."

The beer strike in Sydney is still on. On April 4th, 800 dozen bottles of bottled beer and 540 gallons of draft beer was brought to Sydney by ship **from Adelaide**....

Better news for drinkers. 500,000 bottles of Scotch whisky will become available in capital cities as from today. **This breaks a five year drought.**

Trials of Japanese military are proceeding in Rabaul. The Australian Military Tribunal is finding that many Japanese officers are guilty of **war crimes**, and is **liberally handing out death sentences**. One Army Captain, named Mitsuba, over the last week, has been **sentenced to death on three occasions**, and given 20 years of imprisonment.

Many of the nation's trams have footboards around them. This is a narrow platform that passengers can step onto, in getting on and off. **Fare collectors work their way along the outside of the tram** by standing on these footboards....

A few days ago a conductor was killed when he fell from a footboard. The Tramways Employees Union has called for a **three minute strike** today that will stop all tram traffic for that time, as a mark of respect.

The Federal Government has announced that on June 10, in conjunction with Victory celebrations across the nation, a **medal will be given to each of over one million schoolchildren.** The medal will "symbolise the resistance made by the Australian fighting Services in defending the nation from attack". The medal will be slightly bigger than a penny, and can be worn round the neck

Comment. It sounds silly now, rather like the fridge magnets of a decade ago. But, as a lucky schoolboy who got one, it was quite exciting at the time, and I saw many a schoolyard trade that bargained **one medal for twenty milk-bottle tops**.

The Leader of the **Nationalist Government in China**, Chiang Kai Shek, is hopeful that he can come to an agreement with the **Communist Party**. They are at the moment engaged in hostilities in Manchuria, and it is seen that this **may develop into a wider conflict....**

Comment. This Manchurian situation heralded the Communist Revolution that saw the existing government fall to the Reds in 1949. **If this had been nipped in the bud in 1946, the world now would be a different place.**

The British Government announced that it had signed contracts to import **4,500 tons of rabbits from Australia**. It is happy to take as many carcases as we can provide.

On April 25, the first post-WWII Anzac Day march proceeded though Sydney's streets and celebrated with a ceremony at the Cenotaph. 50,000 men from both wars marched as huge crowds applauded. Other capital cities drew record crowds. **Dawn services in all cities, and country towns also drew record attendances.**

Servicemen who are being held in military detention and who have served **one third of their sentences** will be released if they have been of good behaviour. This includes persons who were AWL, or who were guilty of theft, fighting and insubordination.

WAR BRIDES

In the last few years of WWII, the countryside of England was blessed with an influx of thousands of young, healthy, carefree Australian servicemen, mainly airmen, who spent most nights fighting the "Huns" and, it seems, their spare evenings going to dances. All around them were English roses, beautiful and even younger than these servicemen, excited by war and the freedom it gave them, and easy prey to the derring-do and tragedy that surrounded these young airmen. Inevitably, romances abounded; and many of these led to marriages between what were undoubtedly innocent parties; with the promise that at the end of the War, the girls would migrate to Australia, and settle down to life in the vast Antipodes.

Towards the end of the European War, the Australian and British governments devised a scheme which would facilitate the reunification of these very new families. **Firstly, the servicemen would be repatriated**; "Bring our Boys Home for Christmas" was the popular cry from Australia. **Then**, some four months later, that is when shipping was available, the **brides and the large number of children that the marriages had already produced would be shipped out**, free of charge. Granted the girls would scarcely travel first class. In fact, the accommodation was generally on roughly-converted troop ships, with about eight to a cabin, often without a porthole. The only luggage available to them on board was a single suitcase that must be stored beneath their bunks. Conditions were tough enough, but still, it was free.

Women with children were given first priority, while those who were only engaged to be married were at the tail end of the queue. In this latter case, the serviceman involved had to post a bond of 150 Pounds that would be refunded to him if the couple were married within a few weeks of landing. The first shiploads were sent off at the end of 1945, with others following at about two-monthly intervals, for over three years. More than 10,000 girls took this one-way ride; there was no free passage back for those who opted out.

The trip to Australia took six weeks, and the passengers were trapped on board until they reached Fremantle. The journey through the tropics was sheer hell, particularly for those with children, though at least the food was good after British war-time rationing.

The Book: Overseas War Brides. This charming and informative book, published under the auspices of the Overseas Warbrides Association, contains the tales of 117 brides who made the trip, and who remained here for 60 years when their individual stories were collected for that book. Here, I have tried to report on the typical experience of these brides.

The young ladies were indeed young, many of them still sweet seventeen, who had volunteered for the support Services, or who had been willingly conscripted. They met their husbands-to-be at work, or at the dances that seemed to occupy many evenings. The RAF-blue uniforms cast quite a spell, and when coupled with blue eyes, no-one was safe. Courtships were brief, sometimes only a few months, and sometimes with just a few visits home. The deal to get engaged or married was sealed when the airman got an official notice that said he was to be sent back to Australia in a few weeks.

The families of the brides were worried, to say the least. Their beautiful daughters were proposing to go off 12,000 miles away, to a presumably backward country on the edge of the earth, with a man who was nearly a stranger. There were no jet planes then, only ocean liners, and the journey was expensive and just not on, for most. They thought – rightly in some cases – that they would never see their daughter again. It was so sad.

The young girls – madly in love, and wildly excited – did not dwell on this, and just went. Though now, fifty years later, writing after they themselves have raised children, this retrospective sadness is quite apparent.

Their first glimpse of Australia was Fremantle. They remember the tin roofs on houses, and the boys barefoot – never seen by them before. They got a great kick from eating bacon and eggs in cafes. So much meat impressed them, and the salad on the same plate amazed them. And all that fruit, with the wonder of those exotic passionfruits to boot. They got back on the ship somewhat reassured; the CWA and RSL carers had been wonderful, the natives had not been hostile, in fact, they were quite friendly. The local café-owners must have gone almost broke, giving out so many free meals.

Most of them went on by ship to Melbourne. Some went from there by train to Sydney, and they remember the discomfort of being woken at midnight at Albury, and changing trains, because of **different rail gauges**. Meetings with spouses were generally good, often wonderful, although there was some disquiet at seeing their wonderful war-heroes in standard issue de-mob suits instead of their splendid uniforms.

The meetings with the in-laws were nerve-wracking events, though these generally went well, and the neighbours too were welcoming. But there were exceptions in both cases (see later). Their ultimate destinations spread from Kings Cross in Sydney, to Launceston in Tasmania, to such places as Sawtell and Moree in the NSW bush. A surprising number initially went to small outback farms away from townships, and the isolation there made settling-in all the harder. No matter where they settled, they were all put off by the outside dunnies (complete with the inevitable stories of snakes and spiders), by chip-heaters and wood stoves, and by the lack of refrigerators. And they did not like having to do their own laundry, in coppers of all things – at "home", laundry was simply "sent out".

There were more serious problems. The 1940's had so far seen no homes built in Australia, and most of the existing ones were occupied by the parents-in-law. This meant bunking in with the oldies, and of course this was no more successful then than it has been traditionally. After months, or even years, our brides were relieved to move out, rarely to a new house before 1950, but at least to some independent digs.

An even greater problem was loneliness. They missed their families and friends, and the British countryside, and all things British. And they were lonely because they were not naturally a part of their new communities. Those with children at home found it difficult to meet other young mothers, those on farms were isolated by distance, and some were separated from their only initial support – their husband – by his work commitments. In all, loneliness and the longing for "home" put much stress on the marital relationship in the first five years. But, most survived, and the writers in "Overseas War Brides" almost unanimously still call Australia home.

Exceptions The nuptial blessings did not **always** come from their families. Beryl of Plymouth tells "We married during his brief stay, against everyone's approval, in a registry office in Kensington, completely on our own."

The welcome mat was not **always** out. Olive, later of Kings Cross, tells of her days in Fremantle. "Go home, you Pommy cows" was shouted at her by some Aussie girls on the dockside. Then she met the family. "They hated me on sight." She moved into the in-laws' house. "It was the worst Christmas of my life. I had brought them all presents, which to my knowledge, they never opened."

Peg of Maleny tells of her cold feet. "When I saw him, well, I just wanted to run away. He was wearing civvies and looked so funny, in gear that the Air Force had given him which did not fit him anywhere and a felt hat that looked awful.... I am out of love already. I just can't stand the look of him." Then to make matters worse, she was introduced to his mother. This lady was "wearing a hat I couldn't stand, with a big rose on it ...she looked as if she was going to a garden party..." The reader will be relieved to know that her husband turned out to be "absolutely fabulous."

Brides or sportsmen?   Everyone agreed that it was good to have these brides grace our shores.   But not if the price was too high.   Difficult decisions about priority rose **on two occasions**.

Firstly, the British Rugby League team was due to visit Australia for its first tour since the war. This was a much anticipated event that had a million League-followers salivating over the certain violence of the various fixtures. Should they still come?   Or should they give up their berths to a few dozen brides? After a lot of controversy, it was decided that "after six years of war, the military and civilian populations are entitled to witness a resumption of international sport." So, the tour was on.

Secondly, the Australian Services Cricket team was in the same boat, so to speak. They were members of a team that had been serving in Britain, and was scraped together after the war was over for some memorable matches in England. They were due to revive cricket in Australia with a round-the-nation tour of most of the capital cities. Should they get a berth?

Again, tempers flared. Then it was reasoned that there was really no argument.   After all, they were ex-servicemen serving in Britain, and were due for repatriation anyway. They had a priority greater than the brides, and could thus be shipped on the first available vessel. So, again, the tour was on.

This shared trip, however, **provoked one question that shocked this nation**. One of the brides, named Doreen, of Newton Stewart in Scotland, asked a reporter on board, **"Who is Donald Bradman**?" **Truly shocking**.

Some afterthoughts. About 12,000 **Australian girls**, just as silly and full of fun, went off to America at the same time as our own war brides came here. I can find no reliable statistics on how many of these marriages were successful, but I know of a few that were, and on the other hand, the Press carried many stories of failure. For example, a Press report, under the heading "US Marriage lasts only One Month" went on to say:

An Australian warbride, whose marriage lasted one month, blames mother-in-law trouble for the action her husband is bringing against her. Her husband has charged her with mental cruelty. Mrs Shirley Crush said that her husband had blackened her reputation, and she would contest the suit. She denied the allegation that she had gone to America just for the trip, and that she had had no intention of staying married.

"I would not have waited three years for David if I had not loved him. Some girls might have planned it that way, but I don't want to be classed with girls of such insincere intentions." The suit against her included allegations that she was rude and disagreeable to his friends and relatives. Crush says that her mother-in-law did not like her in the first place, did not want the marriage to take place, and was now trying to break it up. Crush will fight the suit with all her strength.

It is appropriate to mention here that later, from about 1950, there was also a trickle of brides from Japan. From about 1947, Australian troops were among the Occupation Forces in Japan, and were fully enjoying the forbidden fraternization with the local girls. So, again nature took its course, and we as a nation were then confronted with the prospect of Japanese war brides. This is a story that I take up in my **1951** book, but I note here that we did not rise to the occasion. Our government, especially Calwell, was still hooked on the White Australia Policy, and wanted no Asians here at all. And resentment among the population against the Japanese, after the War, was still high. So, combining these with the inherent difficulties of language and culture, our new Japanese brides had a very hard time.

Comments from brides. Speaking sixty-plus years later, members of the Overseas War Brides' Club remembered in particular the shortage of housing. Some of the girls missed the cold weather, and found the hot weather most difficult. "I found the little phone boxes out in the streets most amusing because at home they were always in shops or drugstores (in Canada)." "Our real problem was that there are no washing-machines here; we found weather-board houses difficult after our two story stone houses we all know so well." "We missed our churches such as the 12th Century stone church in Surrey. And sewerage, and nightlife. And no clubs or pubs that we could go to."

Despite their complaints, they gave the impression that they had been happy enough, under strange circumstances. It might have been that those women plunged into remote areas would tell a different story. But as I said earlier, on the whole, the end results for these pioneers were not too bad. Certainly in retrospect, they left no doubt that they now are certain that they made the right choice in migrating, regardless of how their marriage turned out.

WHITHER ANZAC DAY PARADES?

This was the first year since the war that Anzac parades had been conducted. It turned out that this year's parades set the pattern that has persisted, despite varying degrees of opposition to it. Namely, the morning and the march are solemnly devoted to remembrance and meeting old mates, and the afternoon to drinking (by some) and gambling.

Not everyone agreed that this was the way it should be.

Letter, J Myles. My idea of ANZAC Day is that it should be honoured in the spirit of decent conduct. If Australia is ever to rise to true nationhood it will have to banish the wallowing that disgraced our Day of Remembrance.

As an ex-Serviceman of the last War, I want to lodge a strong protest against the complete desecration of ANZAC Day. The solemnity of the morning's act of remembrance is completely dissipated by the drunkenness that follows in the afternoon. Yesterday's scenes were more like a pagan festival for Bacchus than a commemoration of nationhood gained through the blood and sacrifice of the fallen.

This Day has been handed over to the hotels and breweries as an afternoon of swilling and guzzling to wash out all the fine and noble sentiments and exhortations of the morning services and parades.

Comment. One reader responded to this by suggesting that he expected that Mr Myles would be happy if military re-unions were cups-of-tea affairs in the church vestry. Others said that the demobbed servicemen had a lot of shared memories and sorrows that only they could appreciate. After what they went through, the nation should give them one day a year to do whatever they wanted. Many went on to say, that "church biddies and wowsers" should have the sense to stay out of the way on this one day a year.

In any case, on the day of this first post-WWII march, the pattern of solemnity followed by revelry was set for a long time to come.

TEA RATIONING

We in Australia have a lot of genuine institutions. Some of them are held in high respect, like the High Court. Others are perhaps more dubious, like the Parliaments or the Press. But as well as that, in typical fashion, we have many other mock institutions. Don Bradman is one. Saturday night at the Club is often quoted in some circles. But the one which ranks near the top, **the one that was everywhere before the War**, was the great Australian institution of the Cup of Tea. Made from tea leaves, of course, before the days of the tea bag.

Many households, particularly in the city suburbs and country towns, revolved round the great tea ceremony. "Come and have a cuppa", and "wait while I boil the billy", echoed right across the land, millions of times a day. Sometimes the best china was used, sometimes Dad's mug, often ordinary cups – with saucers, of course. Most people appreciated the difference between having a second cup, and having another cup. In a world that moved at a snail's pace compared to today, it was a comfortable ritual that did good service in the tough Thirties.

The Forties and the War changed all that. Tea was rationed, and while the quotas allocated varied over time and circumstances, it was always true that there just was no longer enough. The trouble originated from the Japanese submarines off the coast that insisted on sinking incoming ships, and generally made the shipping of luxuries – such as tea – impracticable. And in later years, the nation was steadily going broke by not exporting enough; so these luxuries were right off the agenda. Half a pound a week was the 1946 allocation to an individual, and that would make about one third of the pre-War usage.

There were no substitutes to be had. Coffee was not grown here at that time. Importing it from South America was impossible, using strange shipping channels; and in any case all available shipping round the world had been requisitioned for the post-war reconstruction effort. There were few other substitutes. Cocoa was in the same boat as coffee. What about Bonox and Bovril? Beef extract? There was nothing. So housewives and their families had to grin and bear it. For years.

In 1946, if the populace had known then that they would be waiting for years for rationing to end, they would have been incensed. But this reality was released a bit at a time; just a hint here, and a shallow promise later. On and on it went, and this was not just with tea, but with everything. In the long run, the housewives' friends removed tea rationing in 1950. A bit late, if you were thirsty in 1946.

NEWS AND VIEWS

Fruit canning. Newspapers reported that Man-Power, the official Employment Agency for the Commonwealth, appealed yesterday for women and girls to help to alleviate Britain's food shortage. "I would be a tragedy if this fruit were lost" said Mr Wall of Man-Power. "Hundreds of tons of fresh fruit are arriving each day at the factories, and will come in by the truck-load for months to come.

"Sydney canneries need between 600 and 800 women workers if Australia is to meet its target of a million cases of fruit for Britain." A special appeal was made for housewives to do part-time work. Wages are Four Pounds a week for girls under 18 years of age, and 13 Pounds a week for those over 18 years.

For Rugby League fans. A blast from the past. The *SMH* reported, as a separate important item, that Test hooker George Watt was **out-hooked** in the Canterbury-Bankstown game versus Eastern Suburbs at Belmore by 32 scrums to 18.

Does anyone else remember what that meant?

New lipstick tinged with blue. Smartest American lipsticks had a tinge of blue in them, Mr Sydney Factor, son of Max Factor, said on arrival in Sydney yesterday. "They are really fuschia tones", he added.

Mr Factor said the latest thing in make-up was "pancake", which although not altogether new, was developed because of its use in Technicolor films, and had become very popular with women generally. "It covers all blemishes; face powder has no colour but, properly selected, is used to give a natural look, according to the colour type of the woman."

American men, he said, were using more amounts of scent and scented talcum powder, and Australian men would follow their lead. Mr Factor expects to be in Australia for more than a year, and he will establish a complete manufacturing plant and sales organisation along the same lines as those in America.

Comment. This cosmetics industry was new to Australia.

Even better good news for smokers. We were told, by **the kindly advertising people at Craven A**, that this brand of cigarette had the remarkable property of preventing sore throats. In fact, they were made especially to do just that. The ad continued with the assurance that not only are they trustworthy, but in fact, they are **thoroughly** trustworthy. What more could you ask?

Comment. Australia was then, and is now, a little behind the USA in a number of matters. For example, US health authorities at this stage were just starting to suspect a link between lung cancer and cigarette smoking. Nothing that anyone could yet prove, but the doubts were there and growing.

Australia had none of these thoughts on our radar, so our smokers were able to enjoy their gaspers untroubled by any such troublesome scare-mongering. What a lucky country we were.

MAY NEWS ITEMS

Weighty issues continued to be **discussed by the UN**. For example, what should happen to **the former colonies of Italy?** No one was particularly interested in taking them over. Should the Ruhr Valley in Germany become a new separate State? Also, the US wanted to impose **a 30-year ban on Japan re-arming**. Or perhaps, **an all-time ban**. There were dozens of hot issues that most of us **in Australia were happily ignorin**g.

The fiction book, *Forever Amber*, was a **reading sensation in America in the 1940's.** Written by American Kathleen Windsor, it told the story of a woman of loose morals who slept her way into better circumstances. The book, based in 17th Century England, was **972 pages long**, though in its initial form it was five times that length....

It was **banned by the Catholic Church world-wide**, and this guaranteed its success. In Australia, the Catholic Church banned it in 1945. In 1946, 84 per cent of the population in the USA said they "read *Forever Amber*." This, in a country with a literacy rate lower than that, was a bit surprising. But it does give an indication of **its market penetration**. The 1947 movie was a big hit in Australia.

Can this be happening? The Minister for Supply announced that he expected that **rubber rationing would be removed later** in the year. That would mean that tyres for cars and tractors and bikes would be available. And sandshoes. Is this a real possibility? Or is it just another Minister getting a blip in public opinion **by holding out false promises**? Remember, **there is an election coming up.**

These were exciting times for some Communists in Australia. About half of Australia's Reds wanted to replace our democracy with a Russian-style Communist state. They hoped to do that by **paralysing the economy of the nation by strikes in major industrie**s....

At the moment, apart from the day-to-day strikes by transport workers and bread carters and the like, **there were major strikes by coal miners and wharfies**. For example, coal rationing was being introduced, and food was rotting on the wharves. 102 ships were stranded at the nation's wharves....

Looking back, it is obvious that such tactics for destroying the nation's economy **would not work in Australia**. At the time, though, it was not at all obvious. So, **the Reds were quite excited**....

Meanwhile, Opposition leader Menzies was quietly polishing up the rhetoric that would allow him to begin his *Reds under the Beds* **scare campaign that won him oodles of votes over 20 years.**

Polio was on the increase across the nation. The Chairman of the Hospitals Commission in NSW said that, although the rise in the incidence of polio was worrying, **there was no need to panic**....

Comment. If there is anything that is more likely to induce panic than the statement "there is no need to panic", I have yet to hear it.

Australia is not the only place enjoying an abundance of strikes. In the US, the nation's entire rail network is closed. In Britain, name almost any industry and it has been shut down by strikes in the last month.

BUNDLES FOR BRITAIN

Towards the end of the War, with a little more shipping becoming available and supposedly more food being grown within Australia, a movement began that encouraged individual Australians to give food to people in Britain. There were two main ways to do this. Firstly, donate it to public appeals such as the Red Cross or Lord Mayors' Appeals right across the nation. The quantities thus received were bulked together and sent to distribution points in Britain. Money was also accepted in lieu of goods, and then used to buy the equivalent commodities here for shipment.

The second way was to bundle up the right type of groceries and send them yourself via the mail, at the same time conforming to various regulations. In this latter case, the parcel could be sent to a specific person.

The various schemes gained widespread popular support, from both corporations and the general public. The collections were considerable, and were well received in Britain. Inevitably, all sorts of disputes about the system developed. But as some of these clippings below indicate, the British public was most appreciative of the scheme, and everyone was deeply impressed by how much was given, often by people who had no specific personal contacts with Britain.

Official statistics, April: Since the inauguration of the Food for Britain Fund in November last year, a varied assortment of food has been sent. It was stated yesterday that the articles sent included 50,976 jars of lemon butter, 352,493 tins of jam, 152,702 tins of meat and vegetable stew, 52,991 tins of plum pudding, 26,106 bars of Sunlight soap, 77,974 cakes of soap, 10,217 tins of camp pie, 1,316 tins of beef extract, and 1,214 tins of malted milk extract.

Many organizations are offering to help the Fund. The net proceeds of a carnival to be held by the Boys' Town Carnival Committee at the Sports Ground on April 7 will be given to the Fund. The Motion Picture Industry is presenting a preview screening of *Spanish Main* at the Regent Theatre, and the entire proceeds will go to the Fund. Admission is by invitation, obtained by subscription to the Theatre. Cash donations to the Fund should be sent to the Food for Britain Fund, 34 Martin Place.

Letters, Ethel Lewis, 37 Campden St, London. It takes a good deal to rouse Londoners, especially at the cinema, where a fairly representative crowd is always to be found. So it was more than remarkable that last week's newsreels contained one item that drew rounds of loud applause.

It was a picture of food from Australia arriving at the docks and being distributed to hospitals and people in badly bombed areas. I saw the same thing happen at a West End super cinema, and a tiny local in Bayswater.

This demonstration was surprising and also moving in a queer way, to one who has had the good luck to encounter Aussie generosity where it grows. Few people here have ever had a chance to realize the kindly affection of Australians for the Old Country. It is the sort of thing hard to describe without being suspected of sentimentality.

But now in another hard hour for Britain, the friends who stood by us in war are ready with help in times of peace. Not the help that bargains, not piece-meal and grudgingly given, but the whole-hearted help of friend to friend from good neighbours the width of the world away. This is what touched our people.

Public eloquence can acknowledge noble gifts of armies and weapons in time of war against a common enemy.

But somehow, when you know that some good soul in Australia is prepared to share her bit of butter with you out of sheer friendship, it seems to ring your own doorbell, and you feel a sense of gratitude that is difficult to express.

Thank God for Australia, we are all thinking here. We are trying to say it from the bottom of our hearts – even where you cannot possibly hear us – in the cinema.

The system had its critics. The high cost of postage was one constant complaint. Another, more serious, was that mailing parcels to specific individuals was inequitable. It meant that lucky individuals could get more to eat than those left out. That of course was **the intention** of the sender. These kind people wanted their **friends and family** to get as many goodies and essentials as they could afford. So the critics, who wanted **everyone** equally to share in the spoils, lost their arguments. In fact, if they had won, it is clear that the good benefactors here would have stopped sending; no one will keep giving stuff to a nameless horde. So nothing came from these complaints, though they did persist.

Another complaint was the opposite. For bulk quantities brought in, it was said they were always given to the wrong groups. Should they be to the hospitals and those badly bombed? Or to expectant mothers? Or to school children? Or even fighter pilots? There was no right answer, and these complaints lingered also.

Letters, A Fell. The Federal Government is concerned, it would have us believe, about the food shortage in Britain, and less concerned about Post Office profits, It should then instruct the Postmaster General to reduce substantially the postage rates on private food parcels. This would enable more parcels to be sent to friends and relatives in the United Kingdom.

Letters, K Watson. Why must the Postal Department limit a parcel for England to 7 pounds. Why is it not 11 pounds, as for clothing? The limit is painfully meager, as those of us know who shuffle round the few tins of food, which seem so weighty. And these few tins have to be divided amongst a family.

Letters, M Milless. I suggest that the Federal Government put the adult population of Australia on the **same food ration for the next year as the British people** have existed on for years, and send every surplus ounce of food to Britain. Extra ships secured to transfer food from Australia could surely be used, on their return journeys, to transport the wives and babies of Australian servicemen.

Deputy Director of Posts and Telegraphs said that Sydney postal officials were handling about **4,000 food parcels for Britain daily**. The volume of business had jumped sharply since the recent announcement of drastic food ration cuts in Britain. Australian postal authorities were unable to do anything to remedy public complaints about the price of postage on parcels, and their limit on total content. The 7 pound limit on food had been imposed by Britain in Britain, and not by Australia. The 11 pound limit on posted parcels was a decision by the International Postal Commission.

The Australian Post Office kept very little of these charges. The remainder went in shipping, freight, and the British Post Office charges for handling and delivery in Britain.

Letter, J Cairncross. In view of the intensity of the food shortage in Britain, it is deplorable that delays in transit and distribution should occur with parcels sent by friends and relatives in Australia. Cable messages yesterday reported that two ships arrived with an accumulation of 150,000 gift parcels. Many of them are long overdue and that "British Post Office workers believe that a large pile must have been built up in Australia awaiting shipment." It is absurd that there should be more complaints of delay now than there were during the war. The postal authorities charge a hefty rate for these parcels, and it is incumbent on them to ensure that the gifts do not deteriorate through congestion in Australia, nor lie undistributed for long periods in British depots.

By August, 1946, the Bundles program settled down. Then, a whole series of statements from British authorities put the cats among the pigeons. And parcels were disappearing from the face of the earth. Where they really went to is anyone's guess. The items below give you some indication of the mayhem.

British Board of Trade, Aug 14: No person abroad may send more than one parcel a month to any person in Britain. Regulations state that parcels must be bona fide unsolicited gifts, and must be clearly marked as gifts. They must not be imported as merchandise, or for sale. Weight must not exceed 11 pound gross, or include more than 7 pound of foodstuff. No one foodstuff must exceed 2 pounds. Parcels that do not comply with these regulations are liable to forfeiture.

Letters, J.A. Mr Simpson, General Secretary of the Food for Britain Fund, says that from the outset people were informed that they could only send one parcel per month to an individual in London. This is true, but what is causing consternation now is the recent announcement that **only one parcel per month may be received by any individual** in Britain, irrespective of different sources of dispatch.

This is quite a different story. How is the sender of the parcel to know if anyone else is sending a parcel to the same person at the same time, and why should not the parcels be delivered, especially if the receiver is the mother of a family.

Let me add that most people here have already contributed to the general "FOOD for BRITAIN" appeal, in some form or other, and they see no reason why their personal gifts should not be considered thus, especially given the exorbitant rates of postage charged. Being "assured" that confiscated gifts are being diverted to a "gift allocation centre" is poor consolation both for the sender of the expensive parcel and the intended recipient, and it is no wonder that **people are losing the urge to send**. Continued interference with gift food parcels can only result in substantial decrease in the number sent.

Letters, D Black. I strongly agree with Mr. Simpson's sentiments. To send parcels involves sacrifices on the part of the donor, not only financially, but also in contents, as one goes without rations, such as sugar, to send them in parcels.

Regulations permit the sending of these parcels, and when regulations are obeyed in every respect and yet still result in confiscation of parcels from the rightful recipients, then this is unwarranted interference on the part of the authorities and is rightfully resented by all.

Letters, B Waterhouse. During the war years – four years at least – I have sent one parcel per month to one address. All through the perils of war, these parcels arrived regularly.

This year, the last four monthly parcels have not been received. I consider these parcels are private property, and, as a British subject, object to their appropriation, whatever the cause.

Letters, Gertrude Spencer, Chipping Norton, Oxon:
Will you allow me to thank those readers who have
written to me about missing parcels.

Since my letter to the *SMH*, inconsistent and rather
muddled statements have come from government departments, ending in a complete volte face by the GPO.
"Many parcels will probably be delivered in the next
few weeks" is one official crumb of comfort, and the
Customs have made **the astounding statement** that
"from January 1, 1945, out of 20 million parcels received from overseas, **only 182 were seized** because of
contravention of government regulations."

Actually, as I personally can attest, some parcels are
now being released. In certain cases, two parcels (posted in different months) have been delivered by the same
post without confiscation; and two elderly women in
our village have received Food for Britain parcels. The
iron curtain has been lifted, and with suspicious speed,
after correspondence and investigation by a section of
the London Press, and Mayor of Auckland's protest.

If Lord Mayors and others officials in Australia made
protests and asked for a thorough investigation at this
end, I believe that your parcels would sail, as it were,
under convoy, and no longer go out unprotected, to be
so often "spurlos versunken" – sunk without a trace.

DO A GOOD DEED

But let me sum up a little. Despite the above glitches, the
benefits from the scheme were obvious, and it achieved its
purpose of making life easier for lots of Poms in a difficult
period. Knowing that, I should offer you the chance to yourself
buy and send a hamper to a friend or relative in England.
Even at this late stage, it will probably be appreciated.

McIlrath's in Sydney might give you a choice. **The first hamper** contains sugar, orange marmalade jam, pastry mixture, a tin of luncheon meat, processed cheese, barley sugar and jelly crystals. **The second choice** adds a plum pudding, and milk powder, while **the third** includes tins of calves tongues and also malted milk, and a bar of Sunlight soap.

The cost in any case would be about one Pound, and there is a money-back guarantee if the parcel is not delivered. But I warn you. You might need to hurry because I suspect that these offers will not last forever.

POLIO

Poliomelitis (infantile paralysis) is caused by a small DNA virus, that exists in the intestinal tract of all humans, but which in some cases multiplies very quickly, and becomes a disease with acute symptoms. Most of the time, a person can become ill for a few hours, and then be immune, virtually for life. For the unfortunate ones, the disease can cause various forms of permanent paralysis and distortion of the limbs, and even death through paralysis of the breathing and swallowing muscles. After World War II, it became obvious that polio was on the increase in Australia, and indeed world wide, and community awareness rose proportionately.

It would be true to say that this was the most feared disease of this period. There was no truly effective treatment, and no cure.

The most dramatic attempt was to place the patient in a respirator called an iron lung, which was efficacious for some, but probably not for others. The disease was halted in its tracks in 1956 by widespread inoculations in Australia using the new Salk vaccine, and then around 1960 by the Sabin oral vaccine. Most patients who had contracted the disease still remained afflicted; there was no retrospective cure for their limbs. But recoveries were possible with early detection. Kerry Packer spent six months as a child in an iron lung. John Laws (a Sydney radio personality) also had a lucky escape.

Until Salk, every parent in this nation had a suppressed fear, each time their child developed some small symptom of illness, that it might be polio. The Salk vaccine was seen as a gift from God and, despite the opinions of a few critics, it remains so.

The articles below capture the concerns of the times.

The Chairman of the Hospitals Commission. There is no occasion for alarm, provided common-sense precautions are observed. Foremost among these is to secure medical attention immediately the slightest suspicion of paralysis arises, for, although the causes are still unknown, much has been learnt of the methods of treatment and the chances of recovery are good provided steps are taken in time.

Letters, A Murray. There is a great deal of concern among parents that their children are vulnerable to the polio epidemic. The fact that the cause of the disease is unknown is most worrying. On the other hand, it is true that there are adequate facilities for treatment, although this is contested by some. It is also true that supplies of special equipment such as iron lungs are currently adequate. Then there has been a very good response for nurses to return to service to combat the disease. So, all of these facts are reassuring. Generally, most of the new reported cases are mild, though there are a large number reported. In all, we can expect that the system can handle any contingency until the epidemic turns down. We believe that medical authorities expect that to happen quite soon.

Public Health Department, May 20: A sharp drop in the number of cases of infantile paralysis is likely over the next two weeks, according to the Department's Deputy Director-General, Dr H Wallace. He said yesterday that the disease apparently came in two waves and the present period appeared to be the peak of the second wave. Usually a sudden rise such as that recently experienced was followed by a sharp fall.

All predictions, however, were more or less guesswork, but were based on developments during past epidemics. Judging from past experiences, **rain did not effect a polio epidemic**. Effects of climate were far from being understood. He added that the resumption of schools after holidays would not affect the number of cases.

The Director-General of Public Health said that the closing of picture shows and theatres had been tried before, but had no effect. A spokesman for a chain of picture theatres said the epidemic had not made any difference to attendances. The Royal North Shore Hospital in Sydney said all its beds were now filled, and they were unable to take new cases. Three other hospitals in the area said they too were full.

Health Department, May 25: Department officials are concerned that **the infantile paralysis epidemic is not abating as expected**. Twenty more cases in NSW were reported to the Department yesterday – **probably the worst day on record**. Total number for the year is now 357. Measures are being taken for further hospital accommodation, and appeals are being made for staff for treatment of the disease.

As a result of an appeal made by the chairman of the Hospitals Commission, Dr. Lilley, ten physiotherapists have offered their services. Two more at present in the Army have offered, and Army releases are being organised. Dr Lilley went on to say that the hospitals were not equipped to serve all patients if their numbers continued to increase.

Teachers' Federation, Jun 5: The Education Department should supply teachers with complete information of the symptoms of polio, a deputation from the Federation, Mr. W. Dickson, said yesterday. The deputation claimed that all milk supplied to children should be in bottles, hygienically sealed. The present method of **distributing milk from cans into cups was described as unhygienic and out-of-date**.

Comment. The sad truth is that, despite some optimistic forecasts in 1946, the numbers continued to rise. By June 1946, there were many suggestions that all schools should be shut for the duration of the epidemic. But common sense prevailed. So the nation sat almost powerless, watching the number of deaths grow, and so too the number of permanently crippled.

The epidemic turned in about 1951, and some five years later the Salk vaccine started to work its miracles. Parents of young children still talk about those intervening years as the most fearful of their lives.

CENSORSHIP

Love me Sailor. This book, written by Robert Close, was reviewed by the Lismore Free Library Committee. The president, Mr C Pitt, announced that it was too bad for men to read, and he would hate to have women read it. The Committee recommended that the copy received by the local library should be destroyed. However, on reflection, they decided to return it to the Public Library and ask for a refund. They would do it with a letter deploring the choice of such a publication for public consumption. This was a prelude to the furore raised that year by the novel "*We Were the Rats*", as described later in this book.

SATURDAY NIGHT AT THE DANCE HALL

I have to hand a programme for a 1946 50-50 dance in the Town Hall at Maitland, a small city in the NSW country.

The first dance was an old-time waltz, followed by a Canadian Three Step. Then a Pride of Erin, and a Fox Trot. The ever-popular progressive Barn Dance, a Jazz Waltz (Ladies' Choice). Violence erupted in the First Set, followed by a Boston Two-step. This was all before half-time.

NEWS AND VIEWS

Forty arrested in two-up raid. Forty people were arrested at Moorefield Racecourse yesterday when police, under Constable Roach, of Kogarah, raided a two-up school, which was in progress. Those arrested were charged at Kogarah Police Station.

The Federal Government has decided to purchase a **20,000 ton whaling factory ship** to be delivered in time for the 1947-48 whaling season. This is the first time that the **Government** has been involved in the industry, although private companies have been operating there for almost a century.

The Department of Trade and Customs was happy to announce that **a special issue of four pounds of refined sugar** would be issued per person to those who wanted it. This was for **the purpose of making jam**....

This special treat was also expected to reduce the consumption of **tinned** jam by Australians, and that **would allow our nation to send more jam to Britain**.

JUNE NEWS ITEMS

The meat ration will be increased by three per cent for the next month. By my calculations, that would give you about a quarter of an inch of fat sausage per person.

The Director General of Health in NSW issued **a warning against the use of talcum powder near the umbilical cord,** because of six deaths of newborns in New Zealand....

He said that jute bags which carried the talc to Australia had been used throughout the war, and apparently were now contaminated. Methylated spirits and petroleum jelly were quite effective as an alternative to dusting. Johnson and Johnson were making urgent enquiries....

Four days later, the Australian Minister for Health said that the tetanus spores found in some imported powder were not found here, and that mothers were quite safe to use it.

Intelligence reports from Japan **say that the bodies of 267 people were found in the streets of Tokyo in April**. They were there as a result of widespread **malnutrition and starvation**.

June 10th. Many nations round the world celebrated this weekend. It was the **first anniversary of the end of the war in Europe**. London's "parade of men and mechanical might symbolised the force that won victory. **A crowd of 5,000,000** watched the colourful parade, their enthusiasm and good humour undamped by the heavy rain. The evening closed with a fireworks display of **unrivalled magnificence." Comment. That figure of 5,000,000 is not a misprint....**

In Sydney, three-quarters of a million people lined the streets. "They gave themselves up **wholeheartedly to**

carnival. Thoughts of the bitter cost of victory, present at the Anzac Day parades, gave place to rejoicing." The **military march** was followed in the evening by fireworks on the harbour and a grand parade of hundreds of vessels. A big success....

One experiment failed. Normally such parades had a number of **bands** interspersed between the marchers. This of course meant that everyone was out of step as the various tunes swirled and ebbed. This time, the decree was no bands at all, **just loudspeakers along the entire route.** They scarcely worked at all, so it was a virtually silent march. Still, the noise and cheering from the crowd made up for this....

But some ex-soldiers had other ideas. At Stafford in England, 2,000 soldiers were invited to march in a local event. Only seven did so. The majority said that **they had finished with parades when they left the army**.

Cigarette papers are essential for the multitude of roll-your-own smokers. They are in short supply. Without them, smokers cannot get the pure taste of tobacco, and this spoils the experience of smoking....

Customs officers across the nation are raiding the premises of rogue printers who are manufacturing bogus cigarette papers, and avoiding the excise payable on them. One raid this week landed a haul of 200,000 papers....

The State executive of the NSW RSL endorsed a suggestion that **ex-Servicemen be given a monthly ration of cigarette papers to go with their tobacco ration** because "tobacco is useless without these papers."

REHABILITATION

After the War was over, for our Diggers there was no quick flit from the Forces. For example, if they were overseas, they could often be engaged in Occupation duties, and then wait months to get a berth on a ship that took weeks to get here. Back here, they were kept in barracks for even longer, and finally demobbed and released into the civilian world. This process took an average of about a year. They were then ready for rehabilitation.

The idea behind rehab was that once people had left the Services, and been outfitted with suitable clothes, they would **ideally** return to their old job and home, find housing soon enough, and move back seamlessly into their old way of life. A whole new book of governmental provisions had been made to facilitate this. Our **Diggers were given suits and clothing**, and while little of it fitted, and none of it was stylish, it got them out of uniforms. Ex-diggers were given **job preference**, which meant that they could get their old job back. But remember that, to take up this offer, they would actually want to go back to that job, and it would still have to be there

It also meant that the current incumbent probably had to leave. In some cases it worked. They were also promised that if they wanted to take up new jobs, then **training would be provided free**. In an appreciable number of cases, this promise was kept. Often, though, these promises, and many others, were just hot air.

Then they were given **preference in housing**. For a given domicile, if the ex-Digger and someone else wanted to lease the same premises, then the Digger would get preference. Given that most applicants were Diggers, this had little effect.

So, in all, the rehab provisions had good results, sometimes. But, equally likely, sometimes they resulted in complete failure. The clippings below show a range of results, and how a few individuals coped.

Director of Re-establishment, June 12: From October to the end of December last, 172,000 men and women had been discharged from the Services, and 131,000 had either been placed in jobs or were in training, the Director said today. There were still about 400,000 to be demobbed, and this was expected to fall to 150,000 by Christmas. The rate of discharge was now at a peak, being at 18,000 per week. Of the 131,000 who had been placed in jobs, 85,000 had gone back to their old jobs.

Comment. Think about those 18,000 a week currently being discharged. **There was no chance at all that they could be properly processed**. Take for example, the matter of getting their old jobs back. **The Army had no idea** if the jobs were still there, or if these war-hardened veterans were still suitable for them. What pay would they be offered, at what locations, with what seniority, and what prospects for promotion? The Army had none of these answers and just **noted that a particular soldier indicated that he would go back to his old job**, and processed him as "returning to previous employment." Granted, that **it was the best that could be done** when masses of personnel were hoping for release at the earliest possible moment. But it was hopelessly misleading to quote the above figures, and to build future policy on them.

Complaints were voluminous. I enclose a small sample below, and these are from **different** parts of the process. But let me assure you that **all** parts of the system were deemed most unsatisfactory by the men now out of uniform, and large numbers of them ended up with a bad taste in their mouths.

Letters, Disillusioned. June 2ⁿᵈ. My optimistic outlook on the prospects offered by Australia to rehabilitate servicemen has been bitterly crushed. I have made more than 50 written applications for positions, ranging from salesman to truck driver, yet not once have I had acknowledgements, or copies of my references returned. I just cannot get a reply.

After being discharged **last September**, I decided to take part in the Ministry of Post-war Reconstruction scheme, and late in October made a written application for a course in journalism. **A week ago** I received a letter saying that my application would go before the authorities for their consideration. So much for the scheme. Now at 22, I am in good health. I am either too old, or insufficiently experienced no matter where I go. I considered opening a business, but found the difficulties insurmountable.

Letters, Alward Windham, Wee Waa. The Herald article on food production states that all restrictions on wheat acreage plantings have been lifted. The actual position is that the machinery of governmental control remains in force with full powers, but with a somewhat friendlier face. Still, before a farmer can embark on wheat production he must secure a licence, and this involves investigation into his qualifications and an interview with the local committee. You can't just buy a farm, and grow wheat. Well, in fact you can, but you cannot legally sell it without the committee's approval.

Getting their approval can take months, and its effect on the two individuals I have known personally has been to cause them to miss the cropping season.

I commend your publicity of the importance of spare parts. When my tractor broke down last November, I found it was one of seven awaiting vital parts at the workshop. I am still waiting, and now reconciled to not sowing a crop this year. Yet in the last year before the outbreak of war, this tractor produced 34,000 bushels of wheat.

As Captain of the Bush Fire Brigade, I was notified of five crop fires caused by defective machines last harvest. Three of these were obviously avoidable if parts had been available. I was fortunate to avoid a fire myself as I did my harvest with a broken exhaust pipe held together with bits of tin and wire. No spare was available, and no workshop within reach could repair it for lack of oxygen.

Special Court report: Convicted in the Special Court yesterday on a charge of having dismissed a returned soldier without reasonable cause, the Nepean Shire Council was ordered to pay 504 pounds.

After a hearing lasting 20 days, the returned soldier Joseph Gow was awarded 400 pounds compensation.

Gow had been employed by the Council as shire engineer in 1915, and joined the AIF in 1940. He was reinstated on his return from war service in 1944, but was later suspended and then dismissed by Council on the casting vote of the president Councillor Rose. Announcing his decision, the magistrate, Mr Bromhead, said it might reasonably be thought that after Gow had served his country, he should have received a generous welcome from his employers. The Council had engaged another engineer, and seemed determined to dismiss Gow. "When Mr Gow announced that he was coming back to work, he was plainly told that he was not wanted but, as the law was, the Council was compelled to employ him. According to the evidence, Gow had instituted proceedings against Councillor

Rose some years ago for 3,000 pounds, and it is now evident that there was a feud between them."

Mr H Snelling, for the Crown, asked for a penalty that would draw attention to the fact that the **law designed to rehabilitate returned soldiers must be carried out by all sections of the community.**

Court report. Despite the recent announcement by the Minister for the Army, a police officer said at the week-end that there was **no precedent for Servicemen to wear uniforms after their discharge**.

In Central Police Court on Saturday, a former AIF solder was convicted and fined 10 pounds **for illegally wearing a military uniform**. The man, said he had been discharged in January. He had been told he could wear his uniform for six months. Mr Sheridan, SM, told Mr Roy that if he wore his uniform again, he must take off the military buttons and badges.

The Minister for the Army, Mr Forde, announced from Canberra last December that servicemen could wear their uniforms, without badges and buttons, up to a maximum of six months after discharge, because of the difficulties in obtaining civilian clothing. **The police view** is that Section 83 of the Defence Act forbids a discharged soldier to wear uniform, and the law must be carried out. It was stated last night that hundreds of men in Sydney were thus offending. Many were waiting for civilian suits to be made.

Mr Forde said at the week-end that he would look into the matter. He would ask the Department of the Army to advise the police authorities of their views.

Hospitals Association, June 15:   The Secretary, Mr H W Simpson urged the establishment of an institution independent of existing mental hospitals for the treatment of war neuroses. He said sufferers were simply drifting on without getting proper care or attention, because of their fearful reluctance to go to Broughton Hall or the mental institutions. Such cases needed their own care facilities. Many cases were allowed to wander in the community without receiving advice, let alone care and attention.

Letters, J Foreshaw. I am glad that you have published several reports recently regarding the treatment of neurotics and what is proposed for these unfortunate ex-Servicemen.

During the past two years, dozens of men have been discharged suffering from war neurosis, without any form of medical treatment. When they applied to the Repatriation Department, they were informed that **a pension was not available for neurosis**, and because no pension was paid, they were not entitled to services.

This meant that dozens of neurotic and psychotic patients have been discharged into civilian life, sick men, left to shift for themselves. I personally sought treatment at Broughton Hall, and underwent "shock treatment", which has proved successful. I later asked the Repatriation Department to pay for my treatment, they replied that they only paid for treatment prescribed by the Department, and that I was not eligible for compensation.

What should be done now is trace all the ex-Servicemen discharged medically unfit suffering war neurosis and who are receiving no treatment, and to ask them whether they have by now received treatment at their own expense, or whether they are still medically unfit.

Letter, John Hedge. I have worked in the coal mines since 1940. When War came, I tried to enlist, but could not, because by then coalmining was a protected industry, so I was not allowed to leave the pits and work elsewhere. Now the War is over, but my pit is still protected, and I still cannot leave. No one will tell me when this will change. How can I plan my life living like this? I can not be replaced by returning miners because those who managed to get into the Army have enough sense to not come back to the pits. So have I, but they won't let me leave. When will this slavery stop?

Letters, Thomas Dart. The ex-Servicemen with land experience, keen to start work to improve his own and country's lot, has been promised aid under (a) the ballot scheme, and (b) the group purchase scheme. Up till now, not one ex-serviceman has been settled under either.

The problem is that agreement must be made between the farmer and the Valuer General's Department, and the VG is offering land that is too small, and does not adequately cover proper water usage. Even if a price is agreed, then every deal has to go to the Treasury for approval, and that will take at least three months.

Furthermore, every farmer needs start-up capital. Land is not enough to get started. We need low-interest loans for a few years to get started. What happens if we get a drought in the first years? If the government is going to give us a chance on the land, they should set us up properly.

Comment. It is easy for me, a long way away from the action, to be not very enthusiastic about the process of rehab. I repeat what I said earlier, that it was probably not possible to do better. Going further back, it also was scarcely possible, at the time of intake, to warn the new soldiers that rehab would be a pain in the neck. That was not the way to recruit for a war.

So, all I can do now is point out that there were some success stories. Granted, the female involved in my story below was used as part of Army promotional literature, so is far from the typical soldier. Still, there were probably more cases like hers, and **only the bad ones made the papers**.

Here is the demob experience of Junee Hall, a member of the WAAF. She had served in the records section of the RAAF during the War, and was now in the process of being discharged. She had recently completed her discharge papers, had her pay-book updated, been given 230 cigarettes, and was just about ready to be demobbed. It was reported that she would take up swimming and tennis. At a professional level, she intends to study music at the Conservatorium; she did not require vocational guidance, and had few rehabilitation problems that were apparent.

When she got her medical clearance, and her clothing coupons for civilian life, she moved off to Woollarah in Sydney, where she was met by her parents. The first thing she did was put on a glamorous evening frock, made for her by her mother.

Comment. (I can't help myself.) Not everyone had it so good.

OVERSEAS NEWS

A bombing in King David Hotel in Jerusalem killed 90 people and reminded us that **trouble in the Middle East between the Jews and Arabs was reaching new heights as the British moved closer to withdrawal from Palestine**.

NEWS FOR SMOKERS

Let me remind you that a great deal of smoking **in Australia was done using roll-your-own tobacco,** and not cigarettes. Groups of men would sit down, say on a romantic stump, and pull out their Log Cabin tins and their packet of Gillette cigarette papers, and slowly **roll their own**. This meant that they always had stained fingers, smelly clothes, yellow teeth, and quickly developed coughs that made quite a dent in their average life expectancy.

The tobacco they used was available legally if it was imported from the USA, but not if grown in Australia. With a few trivial exceptions, all the tobacco used here had to be imported, because of the revenue generated in the Customs Department. So overseas producers like W D and H O Wills cleaned up nicely in this completely protected environment.

But our entrepreneurs were not to be completely denied. Most of them went bush, and started growing their own. So a constant battle was waged between them and Customs. The following newspaper report is typical.

Brisbane, Tuesday. Nine hundredweight of tobacco grown secretly in the Dimbulah district of North Queensland, and concealed in presses in bush foliage, was confiscated by Customs officials yesterday.

Dimbulah is one of the major tobacco-growing areas of North Queensland. This is the third hoard discovered in the last two months.

The latest haul was the result of a painstaking search with the aid of a black-tracker. Six presses for the processing of tobacco have been found recently. Generally, searches had been made through rugged country and under most difficult conditions.

NEWS AND VIEWS

Duke at University: Debutantes to be presented. The Duke and Duchess of Gloucester will attend the University Settlement Ball at the University on April 11, and will receive debutantes in the Great Hall. The debutantes will be restricted to students and the daughters of the Settlement Council. Tickets, at one guinea each, will be restricted to 500.

Comment: Young ladies here no longer make their debut with so much fuss. Also, the venue was described as "**the** university", because, it was **then** the only one in Sydney.

Child competitions. Letters. I hope such competitions such as "the loveliest child" and "**the cutest child**", so common today, will never again be repeated or encouraged.

Nothing but evil can come of them - greed, jealousy, false values, disappointment, and incalculable results on sensitive children, both winners and losers.

The sight of the mothers of these poor contestants is appalling. The depths that they will sink to is disgraceful, including **offering money to judges, and other inducements to male judges**.

News item. The American Broadcasting Company announced that **Bing Crosby** will soon begin **a weekly radio programme** to be broadcast in Australia and America.

William S Hart, the Silver Screen's first **two-gun Western hero**, died on June 25th.

British scientists are **using radar for the first time in history to predict the arrival of storms** up to 10 hours in advance of their actual arrival.

JULY NEWS ITEMS

Supplies of **new golf balls** are expected to reach Australia by **the end of the month**. Adequate supplies of **golf clubs** are not likely for six months.

If you went into David Jones' stores, you would find that you **can buy toast racks, photo frames, and tea trays**. Nothing unusual about this, you might say. But what is odd is they **are made from the laminated plywood of Spitfire propellers**. They are the first to arrive in this country and are reportedly selling fast.

The US military **exploded an atom bomb over 73 ships anchored of Bikini Atoll**. The aim was to gain knowledge of how effective the bomb would be against a fleet....

The results were a little disappointing. Only five ships were sunk, a few were damaged, but most of them simply rode it out. Much of the bomb's energy seemed to go into lifting water into the air, and it then came down as rain....

A few days later the Army announced **that all trial animals within a one mile radius were found to be dying**, from the **"death rays"** emitted. One third of the ships in the fleet were **dangerously radio-active.**

The American Biblical Society will make **films telling the story of the Bible**, chapter by chapter. Three pilot episodes have been made so far. **Out of reverence for Christ**, he will not be shown, but his presence will be indicated by **shadows and footprints**.

Strikes were not always popular with the workers. Many of them, probably most of them, did not want to stop work and lose pay for some trivial cause. But their unions, mostly Communist dominated, called the strike.

If a member resisted, he was often **subject to physical intimidation and, even worse, the reality of being branded a scab....**

This highly contemptuous term would also apply to the family members, and **follow them for life**, no matter where the family might move to. Most often, other union members refused to work with a scab. It was a most useful weapon for a rogue union official....

Justice Brennan in Brisbane said that "I will leave **no stone unturned until the use of the word 'scab' is made a criminal offence**. The word 'scab' must go"....

The world fell on his head, including a personal attack by Prime Minister Chifley. **The term still remains potent in union vocabulary.**

Austerity for the Royals. The traditional pre-war exotic **pastries and raspberries and cream will be absent** from the first **post-war Buckingham Palace formal garden party**. The Food Office gave permission for **only 7,000 persons to attend**, compared to the 10,000 or more pre-war....

Guests will have to be content with **sandwiches and cakes.** Men, who earlier **were compelled to wear a top ha**t, may **this time** attend without. **A sign of barriers breaking.**

July 18th. A *SMH* headline said "**Meat rationing may be lifted by the end of the year.**" **Ho Hum. What, again?**

July 19th. The Minister for Trade said today that the Government **had no intention of removing rationing this year**. "We must continue to ration meat so that we can meet our commitment to Britain."

SANDAKAN

In 1942, after the fall of Singapore to the Japanese, about 1,500 Australian and British troops, all prisoners of war, were shipped to Sandakan on the Northern coast of Borneo. Over the course of the next year, these numbers swelled as more prisoners arrived, until there was a total of about 750 British and 1,650 Australians incarcerated in January 1945.

Conditions within the camp deteriorated during 1944, with mass beatings, deprivation of food and sleep, and almost no medical supplies. Early in 1945, as the US forces drove back the Japanese, a decision was made by the Japanese captors to move the prison camp to a site where more food was available. This involved a march through the mountainous jungle of 260 kilometres to the West, to a site at Ranau.

So from January to August 1945, the prisoners were marched in groups under inhumane conditions until they either reached Ranau, or they dropped dead on the route, or were taken out and killed as stragglers. Those who were left behind in Sandakan, because they were too weak to move, were killed, or simply died from illness or starvation. Those who made it to Ranau were ether executed or died, again from illness and starvation. The last 15 of these were executed on August 27 1945, twelve days after Japan's formal surrender.

The statistics say it all. Of the 750 British soldiers who were thus imprisoned and marched, **none** survived. Of the 1,650 Australian prisoners, **six managed to escape, and no one else survived**. It was clearly one of the worst atrocities ever suffered by Australian (and British) soldiers.

In early 1946, the Australian Forces conducted war crime trials more or less on location. Unlike the Nuremberg trials being conducted at the same time for the European criminals, these trials were not very visible to the Australian public. There was very little newspaper coverage, and indeed they were all over before the public had fully realised that there had been crimes committed. Likewise the families of the victims had been kept in the dark. There never was any public announcement by Government that these Borneo prisoners were being slaughtered, or that the death marches were happening. It was a terrible episode in Australia's history, and the secrecy that surrounded it only made it worse.

About 200 Japanese, Formosans and Koreans were due to be tried by a war tribunal. But about half of these could not be found. Of the remainder, nine were shot or sentenced to be hanged. And half a dozen were given life imprisonment. Nearly all of the others – guilty of murder – were given 10 to 15 years. Here there was another difference from Nuremberg. In April 1952, Australia signed a peace treaty with Japan. This contained provisions that mandated that no further prosecutions would be brought, and this meant that those criminals who had so far avoided capture were now off the hook. And further, pleas for mitigation were now able to be heard, so that even those who had received twenty years were in fact released early.

The following clippings provide a sample of the news stories of the times. They tell about atrocities at Sandakan. Also, there are accounts from other sites to illustrate just how widespread these war crimes had been.

Labuan, Australian Military Court. Two Japanese officers, who were charged with the murder of 824 Australian and British soldiers, were tried today in the Australian Military Court. They were tried in a canvas courtroom, in severe heat, and stoically admitted to crimes that were repellent to all listeners.

Lieutenant Glazer, for the Prosecution, said that Captain Takukawa was ordered by senior officers to close Sandakan Camp and march the prisoners to Ranau, through thick jungle. All prisoners were starving, many were sick, and 400 were stretcher cases. Takukawa ordered Sandakan camp to be burned, and left 28 men to die of starvation and thirst, and took the others away on a ration of **three ounces** of rice per day. Only a few had foot-wear, and the mud was knee-deep.

The march lasted until June 25. Of the 536 marchers, only 183 survived. Stragglers were shot, and their bodies left where they fell. Each morning, men who were too weak to continue were shot. At Ranau camp, the prisoners continued to die, and by August only 133 were alive.

Takukawa decided to kill the survivors. Sergeant Okada asked for the job of shooting the sick. He forced them to crawl to the cemetery, where open graves awaited them. They were shot into the graves. Sergeant-Major Tauji marched 11 men some hundreds of yards away to Tambanan Road. There they were allowed to smoke, while Tauji demonstrated the killing method. Then they were shot one by one.

Takukawa stated to the Court that it was best to kill them because if any prisoner fell out, it would delay the march, and be a burden. His defence was that he was following orders from above. He was sentenced to death by hanging, and his adjutant, Captain Watanabe, received the lesser penalty of death by firing squad.

Hanging of Japanese soldiers: "Two Japanese captains, Takuo Takukawa and Susume Hoshijima, were hanged at Rabaul yesterday for the murder and cruel torture of hundreds of Australian soldiers during the death march from Sandakan to Ranau, British North Borneo, in 1945. The condemned Japanese asked for drugs, but the request was refused".

Takukuwa, as he was led to the scaffold, was heard to heard to mutter in Japanese: "I will pray for the Emperor." A green handkerchief was placed over his eyes, and his hands firmly handcuffed behind his back. A second later, the trap was sprung, and the Japanese who had been in charge of the death march and who was known to have massacred 33 unknown prisoners of war, tumbled to his death. The English-speaking Hoshijima arrived under close provost escort. As he approached the 13 steps to the scaffold, he shouted: "Long Live the Emperor."

OTHER MASSACRES

There'were other atrocities reported to the various military courts.

Massacre of wounded: At Parit Sulong on January 22, 1942, from 250 to 300 wounded men, left behind by the British and Australians who escaped under Lieutenant-Colonel Anderson, across the river, were massacred in cold blood. On January 13, 1942, Japanese soldiers entered the Alexandra Base Military Hospital, and shot or bayoneted 183 patients and 143 doctors and other medical personnel.

Batch Shootings: In Singapore, on January 23, 1942, nine Australian soldiers and some civilians had their hands tied together and were blindfolded. They were then shot in batches of three, tied together. Some of the victims were taken from a Red Cross truck. In Timor, four Australians had their throats cut. And were hanged. Another eight were tied together by the wrists and shot at close quarters.

Nurses Machine-gunned. On February 14, 1942, in the Banka Straits, the Japanese drove into the sea and machine-gunned a number of men and women, including 23 Australian nurses, who had previously surrendered. One of the nurses, Sister Vivian Bullwinkel, survived and, having completely recovered, was able to give a full account. Some measure of her travail can be gained from the stage play *"The Shoehorn Sonata"*, now occasionally played in Australian theatres.

Comment. The soldiers and nurses and others who died or survived during this period are the greatest heroes that it is possible to imagine. Young and older, they went away with a song on their lips to what they thought would be an adventure, to fight a foe that was as bad as could be. They were killed and maimed and tortured and starved and imprisoned and beaten in the most horrible way. They deserve our eternal gratitude.

SHOPPING

Shopping in 1946 was a pretty mundane affair. In the suburbs and country towns, the woman of the house went to a smallish cluster of shops in some central spot, and bought enough groceries and what-have-you's for a few days. She got the meat at the same time, although bread, ice, and milk were delivered to the home. So too were fruit and veggies, and maybe fish, and maybe rabbits. If anything was needed on an ad hoc basis, say a bottle of Scott's Emulsion, some of the bigger children walked or rode a bike down to a corner store.

Every now and then, Mum would gather up her flock and head into a city, and buy clothes and shoes, and things for the house. And perhaps a dress for herself. Some few were lucky enough to get to the big Department stores in the major cities, but the lady from Condobolin knew nothing of this thrill. Farmers, David Jones and Mark Foys were well and truly on the scene in the cities, and provided the level of sophistication that smart ladies and gentlemen needed.

These latter also provided **mail-order catalogues** that were really quite successful, bringing city finesse to the country area. Shops closed at five o'clock, except for milkbars, and petrol was also hard to get after that time. Doctors closed their surgeries early in the evening, but, mind you, they did a lot of their business through house calls.

There were as yet no thoughts of malls and magnificent car parks. Even regional shopping centres, spread round the outer city suburbs, had not yet been hatched. But, to make life worthwhile, ladies' fashions were starting to come back to the glitter and gloss of the pre-war years as garments trickled in from overseas. Though, inevitably, only if the lucky lady had – or could get – enough coupons.

In 1946, the hottest shopping topic was **the question of zoning**, because the war-time home-delivery system was now under question. This had been foisted on an unsuspecting population at the start of the War, ostensibly to prevent wastage of manpower and materials. It applied to bakers and butchers, and fruitos and icemen, and grocers and anyone who home delivered. All of their trading areas were each split into zones. Every customer was allocated to a zone, and that meant that all the households in that zone were at the mercy of the one baker or butcher; and that person could deliver only in his designated area.

Since customers were to be serviced by the same baker for years and years, it is not surprising that frictions developed, and that cries for more competition were common. There was still **no possibility of price competition**, since **prices**

were fixed by the Federal authorities, but different levels of service were possible.

In mid-1946, a major campaign to abolish zoning was organised by the Housewives' Association, and the papers were full of complaints. Protest meetings were widespread. Some women were very attached to their bakers, and in fact, some of them loved them. Others hated their butchers. On the other hand, the deliverers wanted zoning to continue. So, there was much to-do.

Recently, the Federal Minister for Post-war Reconstruction said zoning was terminated. This was quite nice of him, since it was the States that regulated such matters. And the States, quite surprised by **this unenforcible announcement**, were simply not ready to revert to a system that might not make sense. So that everything in reality went into limbo while everyone scratched their heads, and said different self-serving things.

Letter, Trade Associations.   Although **regulations** providing for the zoning of bread, milk, and ice deliveries will be revoked immediately, **the practice of zoning** will continue in some form indefinitely by the traders concerned. Representatives of the milk vendors and bakers said last night that when zoning was abandoned, prices would be increased.

Two officials of the Milk and Ice Carters' expressed contradictory views on the question of deliveries by members outside their zones. The executive of the Bread Carters' Union decided last night to instruct members **not** to deliver outside their zones, pending a mass meeting which would be called immediately.

While all this confusion persisted for a month, the letter below expressed nicely the thoughts of a vendor who was not at all keen to get back into the dog-eat-dog world that might develop. This letter explains why.

Letters, Jackie Lord. Early in the War, we bakers had been forced to set up a zoning system. The operation was not an easy one. A committee of four or five was set up. Maps had to be produced, showing every street and lane, from Cook's River to National Park beyond Sutherland. Every street had to be visited. And every house counted in the whole of the area. Then these had to be formed into zones to approximate as nearly as possible the trade that each of us 50 or more bakers engaged in the area had been doing under the old system.

To accomplish this, members of the committee worked day and night for about three weeks or a month before the plan was in workable condition and right throughout the customers' interests were taken into consideration.

At one stage it was suggested that depots should be set up and that people should come here for their bread. We considered the aged people, who would find it very difficult to walk any distance for their bread; also the housewife who had no children to send, and, most of all, the expectant mother. We decided that the bread must be delivered daily, and it has been delivered daily, and at times in teeming rain. Yet the Housewives' Association unjustly drags bread zoning into the picture because the butcher and grocer do not deliver.

In my own little business I had to purchase land for a horse paddock, build stables of brick to council standards, buy horses and carts, and let my motors lie idle and deteriorate. My first petrol ration was 140 gallons a month. At the end it was 12 gallons a month.

After the sacrifices we have made, is it fair and just to expect us, on the whim of a very few, to give our horses away, or sell them for cats' food, or feed them for nothing, and get our motors rushing and tearing all over the place like old times. Master bakers should be given ample time to get back to peace-time business. They should retain bread zoning in its entirety at least until the end of 1946. This will give us time to adjust

After about August, zoning was gradually abolished. After all the excitement the issue caused, it was all something of an anti-climax, with many customers still sticking with their existing deliverers, and many others just having no new source of competition anyway.

At the same time as the zoning controversy, shop retailers became intent on getting rid of **competition from fruit barrows in the city**. As is customary, they did not attempt a frontal attack by saying that barrows with their low overheads were posing a threat to themselves. Rather they were suddenly very concerned with the dangers to motorists that the barrows now presented. A more legitimate concern was for **the horses that pulled the barrows**.

The Secretary of the RSPCA, Mr W Painter, expressed alarm at reports he had received of gross cruelty by city barrowmen to their ponies. If necessary, inspectors from the Society would patrol all day to ensure that the ponies were properly treated, he said. No further notice would be given nor excuses accepted, and prosecution would be immediate.

Ponies are forced to stand in the sun all day without food or water. "I have even heard of pineapple ends being tied to the shafts to keep the ponies going", Mr Painter said. Most of the offences were the result of thoughtlessness. Some carts were loaded with all the weight in the rear, making it difficult for the horse to stand.

News item. **NSW Womens Justices' Association** protested today against a suggestion by the NSW Fruit Shopkeepers' Association to **limit the number of barrows selling fruit.** "This is an attempt to create a monopoly in fruit buying at the markets for members of the association", said Mrs D Fahey. "Long live the barrowman who is reducing the price of fruit and vegetables in Sydney. I am surprised that these men do not have an association of their own."

NEW PRODUCTS ON THE SCENE

Then there were little luxuries which had been taboo for so long. For example, **cultured pearls.**

Advertorial.   We have just realised that a cultured pearl **is** a real pearl. It is the same satiny smooth fluid that an oyster secretes when a tiny speck gets inside his shell and irritates him, so that he covers it with pearl. But with cultured pearls, you don't wait for chance to wash a grain of sand; you make sure by popping a wee grain of mother-of-pearl in. And then you have to wait seven years for the oyster to do his stuff. Result is – a real pearl. All of this apropos Elizabeth Reimer's announcement of the first cultured pearls to arrive for years. She's had some of them set in 14ct gold. Rings, necklets, earrings. Strings from £27 to £250.

Now for something that you have had in your house for ages, and thought always existed. Well, here below the standard can-and-bottle-opener makes its Australian debut.

Advertisement. What is a post-war kitchen without a good, shiny, little bottle-opener? So, just to remind us that the War is over, McCathies show us a first-rate little gadget which only robs you of four-pence halfpen-

ny. Its called the Quality, and we'll even forgive it that
so handy is it. It opens tins quickly and cleanly, whips
corks out in a jiffy, and neatly removes those metal
bottle-tops which **ruin all your forks**. So there you are.
Snap down to their basement in Pitt Street.

NEWS AND VIEWS

Letters. A whispering campaign is operating in England
to block the selection of that great English cricketer, Walter
Hammond, as captain of the next English team to visit
Australia.

It is said that Hammond would not be a good ambassador, as
he is not a good after-dinner speaker. Of course, **the trouble
is that he was once a professional, and is now an amateur**.

There are many previous captains who could not make an
after-dinner speech. For example, W G Grace, on a tour of
Canada, on 17 occasions told hosts that he appreciated their
hospitality, and hoped it would continue as the tour went on.
That was his only message.

In any case, back to Hammond. We would hope that captaincy
will be decided on ability to bat and lead, and not on speech-
making. And certainly, **not on whether he has accepted
money to play in the past.**

Comment. Professional cricketers were still frowned on in
Britain. Even when visiting Australia, they came and went
to the field through separate gates, from separate dressing
rooms.

Remember: Nestles penny chocolates, red and white striped
bulls eyes, and sherbet bags with licorice straws?

Rockdale Council report. The Council last night refused
permission for a number of live fowls to be released from

the highest convenient position on the local town hall tower, which is 60 feet high, to publicise a Youth Campaign appeal at the end of April. Alderman Jones said the idea was ridiculous and was of the opinion that if it had not come to the Council officially and on business paper, he would have thought the applicant was having a pot at them. **He added that poultry and eggs are too scarce these days.**

The Deputy Town Clerk, Mr Town, was deterred by the mess that would be created by the stunt.

Prisoners of War.   This release from the British Navy serves to remind us that Germans were also kept as prisoners-of-war, and also that they were still not released a year after the War in Europe was over.

Aboard the US ship *Frostberg Victory*, 150 of the German prisoners were found to be sick when it anchored in the Mersey. Investigations showed that the prisoners had heard that they were to be sent to Russia, or made to work in mines. Many of them ate soap or drank diesel oil to make themselves sick and a small number were taken to hospital. Most of them were in fact brought to Britain to work on English farms.

Cairns, on the coast in northern Queensland, is under invasion. **It will soon hold an auction of 50,000 tons of army surplus goods** left over from the war. Accommodation is booked out, and bidders will be accommodated in disused army barracks.

Rationing was lifted on new car tyres. Distribution depots were in the cities, so country areas would not get immediate benefits. In fact, Dunlop estimate that **the pent-up demand would last till the New Yea**r.

AUGUST NEWS ITEMS

Beer in pubs is currently sold in NSW in 16 ounce glasses as a schooner, and 9 ounces as a middy. The new Liquor Act provides that these be replaced by 20 ounce glasses selling as a pint, and 10 ounces as a half-pint....

There are problems. Due to a shortage of glass, **it will take one year to get the glasses**. Then, the increase in volume on these new measures would mean an increase in price. **The Prices Commission would probably not allow this**....

Beyond that, **messing around with beer supply is a tricky political issue**. Everyone agreed that "the working man must have his beer." With Federal elections coming up on September 28th, this was a hot subject.

The international trade in brides goes both ways. Some 650 excited Australian brides of British servicemen arrived at Britain's Plymouth on the aircraft carrier *Victorious*. The girls were warned by the Captain, before leaving Perth, that anyone who "misbehaved would be **put ashore**." Given that no alcohol was allowed, and that fraternisation with the crew was strictly controlled, **no one was marooned**.

Immigration Minister, Arthur Calwell, presented details of his plans for **admitting immigrants into Australia**. He said that about **100,000 persons had already applied**, and he expected that many more would do so soon. Of these, **90,000 were from Britain**, and the rest from Europe....

British ex-servicemen would be given top priority. 4,000 of these had applied. Next would be persons who brought **work skills** needed in this nation and who also could make

their own arrangements for housing. Europeans would also be eligible on the same basis. Asians need not apply.

Many thousands of **British troops were stationed in Germany** to preserve peace and assist in reconstruction. They were **the victors** and wanted their wives and families to join them. To make room for them, **thousands of German families were being evicted** from their dwellings. German women were protesting in small mobs against this....

They were doubly incensed because **German prisoners-of-war were still being held "in slavery" in Britain** as workers on farms. **Comment. For the losers, Peace was not bringing much peace there.**

Coal miners here were causing much chaos in industry by short-term strikes. The coal owners were doing their best to increase profits by not recognising that **war-time conditions would have to be improved**....

Miners were seeking **three weeks annual leave** (rather than the current **two**) and to be **paid sick leave**. They also wanted to be **paid weekly**, instead of fortnightly....

Comment. It is easy to forget that **many workers, did not have paid sick leave**.

General MacArthur, as Supreme Allied Commander in Japan, has granted **that** country **the right to harvest whales in the Antarctic**....

This was strongly opposed by Australia, which was itself in the process of setting up a whaling industry. This is the **start of whaling disputes between Australia and Japan** that have lasted till the present day.

SOME PROBLEMS FOR MEDICINE

Too many doctors. The **British** Medical Association (BMA) was the representative body that spoke for doctors in Australia It was not until 1962 that the Australian Medical Association was declared an independent body. Back in 1946, the BMA had a problem. The nation was facing a surplus of doctors. The number of students entering the profession was showing a large post-war jump as **ex-military took up their rights to training**. So, the universities were being flooded with ex-diggers who want to swap their rifles for scalpels.

State Branch of BMA. Restrictions on the entry of students to the Faculty of Medicine at Sydney University appeared to be the only way to avoid what might be a serious surplus of doctors, the Secretary, Dr John Hunter, said last night.

If students continue to enter medicine at the present rate, there will undoubtedly be more doctors than the community requires. At present, there are 600 in first-year medical training alone. The total for the first three years would probably be 1000.

These are abnormal figures, and far exceed the ordinary requirements. Parents will have to decide whether it is worthwhile for their children to enter medicine with its long years of training and the possibility, perhaps, **of very little return at the end**.

Dr. Hunter said that normally the NSW community needed 40 to 50 new doctors each year. Country districts might be able to absorb more if the medical practitioners were assured of a reasonable income.

There were other worries inside the medical industry. The Chairman of the Hospitals Commission, Dr Lilly, said that practically every hospital in Sydney and in the country is still suffering from **a desperate shortage of trained nurses**

and domestic staff. As a result, many hospitals are unable to use beds for which there is an urgent demand. Long hours of overtime worked by nurses to keep hospitals going have led to widespread complaints. Although the ManPower authorities are giving priority to hospitals with women seeking employment, the shortage is expected to persist for at least a year.

He added that the shortage is a natural aftermath of the war. It has reached these proportions because for five years of the war, young women from whom nursing trainees normally would have been drawn, had entered the women's services and they were not back yet. Normal conditions in which girls of 18 would look to the hospitals as a means of entering an important and dignified profession, had not yet returned. It is assumed that most of these are having a well-earned holiday, and when this is over, will again seek re-employment. Others had married and have given up their profession for good.

Dr. Lilley stated that the system of training nurses in NSW could be overhauled with advantage to the hospital system and to nurses generally. He considers that trained nurses with considerable experience should be more adequately paid, but that conditions for trainee nurses **compare more than favourably** with the conditions for girls of a similar age in other industry.

Dr Lilly **might** have been correct in this latter statement. But this announcement from Sydney Hospital tells us that nursing was not a great job, at least by today's standards.

The reduction of nurses' working week to 44 hours, which came into effect today, would, it was hoped, attract more trainees into the profession, the President, Sir Norman Paul, said yesterday.

Comment. Over many years, nurses have struggled to get better conditions. But it seems that they always have to do battle for everything they get. It would be nice for them to get the occasional free kick.

THE FIGHT AGAINST TB

In the latter part of the year 1946, tuberculosis (TB) became a community concern. It had long been a major killer in Australia – about 3,000 deaths per year – and, postwar, the incidence seemed to be on the increase. Yet Governments at all levels appeared to be indifferent to this, and even **promises** of action were hard to extract. But the facts were that TB had become **the leading cause of death for persons under the age of 45.** It was causing four times as many deaths as all other infectious diseases put together. Despite this, Australia's per capita expenditure on TB was miles behind that of Britain and the US, and only ten percent of that of Canada.

The tragedy was that while TB was a contagious disease, it could be eradicated by the provision of decent food and shelter, and by early detection, and by the provision of proper hospitals and nursing, and by the temporary isolation of patients from others. None of these was being funded effectively by our government.

In NSW, in 1944, the Government made two flamboyant gestures. **Firstly**, it promised the princely sum of two hundred and fifty thousand pounds to provide a food allowance for sufferers. **Secondly**, the Minister for Health, Mr Kelly, spoke of a million pounds for "a scheme that was being prepared to wipe out TB in NSW". As the *SMH* editorial put it, "**further pipeclay promises.**"

The same Mr. Kelly put his foot in it in November, 1946, in a most spectacular manner, when **he blamed the epidemic on**

the shortage of nurses. The public response to this was fast, furious and widespread.

For example, the *SMH* in an editorial elaborated on six prominent Sydney private TB hospitals that had no trouble in remaining fully staffed. It went on to talk of an excellent facility in Newcastle that had never opened because of a staff shortage. The *SMH* asked **"Has the Department of Health really tried to collect a staff?** No advertisement for staff ever appeared in the Press". It went on to decry other efforts at providing relief. For example, it pointed out that "Over six months ago, a TB Advisory Committee was formed by the Minister. **It held a preliminary meeting**, and has not met since. Nor is it possible to ascertain when, if ever, it will meet again."

A second *SMH* editorial continued the attack on Mr Kelly. "It would appear that the basic remedy has not occurred to the Government. That is, to make the profession of nursing and conditions of hospital work more attractive." It pointed out that wages were poor, that junior nurses were not only compelled to live-in, but that living conditions for them were notoriously bad. "Today, after a long and protracted training, a qualified nurse receives no more than a woman who is at best trained for only a few weeks." Better wages and conditions for nurses will relieve the tragic plight that sufferers now experience, it said.

Comment. Mr Kelly's stance elicited more abusive Letters than any other issue throughout the entire year.

There were other sides to this story.

Letters, B Milliss. As Vice-President, of the Macquarie District Assembly, I visited Queen Victoria Sanitorium on Friday afternoon, and found that Mr Kelly's information was not in accordance with the facts.

Conditions were far from satisfactory. These are some salient points:

One ward containing six beds was closed last year. Broken windows and need for internal repairs made it unusable. Staff shortage was not the cause of the closure. Two single rooms were also unusable. The general need for repairs includes broken doors. There are no separate nurses' quarters, or accommodation for additional nurses. One member of the domestic staff is using a room normally occupied by a patient.

The dining-room roof leaks, and the paint is peeling off the walls. A carpenter arrived recently, but went away because he could not get materials for repairs.

Wards lack lockers and there is only a common room for suits and overcoats. The wards inspected were bare and dreary. The depressing psychological reaction on a well person conveys some idea of the harmful effect on the unwell.

The patients' laundry is an 8 by 10 room with two cement tubs, and cold-water tubs. An electric iron point and table are the only other conveniences. The house laundry is without hot water. Certainly, Mr Kelly cannot get a correct perspective from his office in Pitt Street.

G McCready, Assistant General Secretary of the NSW Nurses Association, says part of the problem is the resentment of people to sanitoria in their own areas. This, of course, is to be expected. No one wants to have a centre for a highly contagious disease next door. The solution, he went on to say, is to legislate for longer holidays for nurses, provide them appetising and nutritious food, and regular testing for the disease.

Letters, B Cowan. Australia is lagging badly in the control of tuberculosis, which still holds first place as the destroyer of young lives. In the past 30 years, Australia has lost well **over 100,000 of its best citizens through death from TB**, a disease which could, and should, be prevented. If we are not moved by the humanitarian aspects of this great problem, by the sickness and suffering and despair which it causes, perhaps we might give some thought to the material side of the matter.

There is no better opportunity than now for the final conquest of TB. The way is well defined, the measures necessary for its control are known, comprehensive plans have been formulated, and have been presented over and over again to responsible authorities, but the greatest difficulty is getting any part of these plans implemented. It is fashionable to blame lack of action on difficulties caused by the war; but these conditions have always been with us and will continue to be unless someone stirs.

The control of TB is a Government responsibility; this is a communicable disease, a social and economic problem, just as much as it is a medical one. All Governments, Federal and State, Labour and Liberal, have been at fault for their lack of vision and lack of concerted action against this enemy within our gates.

In NSW, the most urgent need is for another 1,000 beds in modern chest hospitals and sanatoria, where the care and comfort of the nursing and domestic staff, as well as the effective treatment of patients, will receive full consideration. Clearly a competent guiding hand is needed to give force and direction to the campaign for the eradication of TB in Australia.

There were also many Letters telling tragic personal stories.

Letters, TB SUFFERER. I quite agree with your article about TB sufferers having a raw deal. This is my story: I have been given what is, I expect, a death sentence.

Last week, I came to Sydney to seek advice concerning my chest condition (I have had TB for six years). At the hospital clinic, I was told an operation would arrest the disease, but that I would have to wait about six months, as there were many ahead of me. In the meantime, I would have to rest, as the opposite lung now shows a spot which will otherwise spread, and if so, nothing can be done.

I was given a note to go to Waterfall for this rest period, but at the Board of Health, I was told I would probably have to wait two years for a bed there, as I had been there before, and others must be given a chance (and they have to wait months anyway).

So now I have the alternative of waiting in Sydney, staying with a sick aunt and doing housework, or going back to my husband's farm, where it is very hot in the summer, and where I can't rest, as he can't stop work to look after me. I am only 25, and I have tried very hard to get well, but now it seems all my efforts are in vain. I wonder how many other Australians are in the same predicament?

There were plenty of similar Letters. A Sydney writer, calling himself **SPECIALIST,** told of a young patient of his who needed a specialist surgical operation to collapse a diseased lung. "His name was entered on a waiting list at one of our leading hospitals. He was still waiting for a bed sixteen months later … and recently he died. Apart from the tragedy of his own death, he probably infected others while he remained at home."

A second writer**, ANOTHER SPECIALIST**, also from Sydney, tells of a similar case, and goes on to say:

The writer of your article has shown that, for the years 1914-1945, more Australians were killed by the tubercle bacillus **than were killed by the enemy in two major**

wars. Even this, of course, is not the full story. The bald figures take no account of the family of a bread-winner suddenly afflicted with the disease, **forced to exist on a pittance just adequate to sustain life**, with the children deprived of such elementary necessities as fruit. Statistics do not depict the case of the chronic sufferer, perhaps lingering for years, a burden to himself and, perhaps, infecting several others in the household before death finally ends his course.

Comment. For TB, as with polio, the long term solution was through vaccines. In terms of TB, some relief from the epidemic was afforded by better sanitation, and from isolation. But it both cases it was the vaccines, BCG and Salk, 10 years down the track, that did the trick.

Venereal disease. Venereal disease was present in high rates, especially after the servicemen returned from overseas. Education about avoiding venereal diseases was much less than that made available now for AIDS, largely because it was just not done to talk about these things. Also, men and women were not in the habit of using contraceptives; and of course, such bodies as the Catholic Church forbade people from doing so; as indeed they still are forbidden.

Warnings of the dangers were given liberally to the armed forces during the war, and started showing up in 1946, in the major dailies, for the civilian population. Such notices were major breakthroughs, removing the various taboos that society placed on discussions of this major scourge. Typically they gave a message such as this.

How much do you know, son? You're no fool. You know more than your father thinks you do. But are you quite sure you've got your facts straight?

Start with this. It isn't smart to break the rules of moral conduct, and gamble with the hope of getting away with it. It is shoddy, cheap, -- and deadly dangerous.

There is only one sure way. **The way of chastity.** And if in doubt about this deadly disease, get medical help immediately. It is the only thing to do if **you are not man enough to live cleanly**.

Comment. A few years later, this softly, softly approach was gradually replaced with tougher and more direct messages about the consequences, and the links to the very serious medical conditions that the diseases could bring. Gradually, though, relief was somewhat achieved by the slowly changing attitudes to contraception.

In 1946, an incipient lover would sidle into a chemist's shop and wait for a male to serve him, and then whisper that he wanted a packet of French Letters for his brother. This attitude changed, as society became willing to talk more openly about sex, and so slowly, very slowly, the effects of VD were reduced. Until of course, AIDS came along in the 1980's.

Road deaths. In 1946, there were far fewer cars on the roads then, and drivers went at a slower pace. And, it is true to say, people were not in such a hurry as now. Still, in the balance, roads now are much better that they were then. So, the total number of road deaths and injuries was not all that much different from later figures.

But the pattern was quite different in **that pedestrians suffered higher incident rates**. When we drive today, there is a general acceptance that the car is king, that pedestrians have little place in the same space. Back in 1946, a lot of citizens had a general contempt for a lot of rules that we now accept as part and parcel of our living. So, many of them were careless when it came to traffic regulations; and this showed up in the statistics. Of course, many more people walked than they do now, so the figure is perhaps not so surprising. In any case, it is interesting to see that **the emphasis of blame was on pedestrians, rather than today's focus on drivers**.

NEWS AND VIEWS

Changed attitudes to divorce. On July 7, 1946, an Irene Basman was granted decree nisi on the ground that her husband had been in a relationship with another woman. The other woman was listed as **co-respondent** in the court lists, and later the Court found in favour of the ex-wife in the disposition of all property. Then a Kit Marshall was found to have been guilty of **adultery**, and similarly treated. It is interesting to reflect on the term **adultery**, because it now seems to be almost dropping out of our vocabulary. Likewise, how many **co-respondents** have you heard of recently? All of this changed a lot when Geoff Whitlam came to power in 1972, and he legislated for no-fault divorce. In any case, in the past the rules pertaining to divorce were a lot tougher than they are now.

Remember too another matter that has almost completely disappeared. **Breach of promise.** In August, a Supreme Court judge awarded 125 Pounds to a lady from Maroubra, the plaintiff, in an action for breach of promise against a man from Kensington. I think that in today's courting scene, where relationships can come and go quickly, it is just as well for the Court system that the offence has lapsed. South Australia started the ball rolling on this by formally abolished relating laws in 1971, and actions now in other States under the Common Law are few and far between.

Smuggling. This is a strange social issue. But the black market under rationing was so profitable that all manner of goods were smuggled all over the place. Here, we see that even **the beautiful South Australian whiting** was not safe.

News Item. Large scale **smuggling** operations of **SA whiting**, by Victorians in South Australia, have been revealed by a swoop by special investigators of the Price Commission at Thevanard. Persons involved will be prosecuted.

Inspectors said the black market prices in Victoria were 10 shillings a pound, while the official price was four shillings and fourpence. Also, they said, SA whiting travelled much better that other species. During the spying operation, inspectors camped out for more than a month, living off tinned food. At one stage they all got ptomaine poisoning. Similar pouncing operations were held at various locations along the west **coast of SA**

Bottled Beer shortage. Letters. Some months ago, when beer rationing was supposedly finished, workers thought they would be able to get a better supply of bottled beer to take home, but **today the position is worse that ever**.

All sorts of excuses are made by the Melbourne breweries – shortage of bottles, corks, malt and sugar – but the breweries are sending huge shipments of bottled beer to Queensland. Last week the steamers *Fiona* and *Beltana* took large supplies away, and 500 cases went to Hobart. In Queensland, there are at least four breweries, three of which are supplied with malt also from Victoria.

Can the Australian Shipping Board explain how space is allocated to beer, when urgent oats and chaff are shut out for starving stock from Queensland?

The beginning of the Licensed clubs as we know them. A report out of NSW Parliament announced that 99 new style licenses would be granted to community Clubs in the near future. These are quite distinct from those currently available for the City's nightclubs. They will introduce, into Australia, drinking conditions that the English are familiar with. Ninety nine new licences will be granted, 30 in Newcastle. They will be granted mainly to ex-servicemens' Clubs, and at least one will be given to each electorate.

Brighter Sundays. Letters, W Gordon Sprigg, Sunday Christian Observance Council. Many thoughtful citizens believe that Sunday should stand for liberty to worship God unhindered by the temptations and attractions of the week day.   The so-called "brighter Sunday" which it is claimed would appeal to overseas tourists, is not, as far as can be ascertained, in any way a British feature; on the other hand, the English Sunday is the coveted and precious heritage of the British people.   After all, it is the residents, and not the tourists, who should decide such matters.

Cannot the Lord Mayor of Melbourne see his way to use his position and influence to check the growing deterioration of the sacred day and assist to guide right action?

Comment. Melbourne was notorious for its **Sundays showing no sign of human life**.

Seven adult members of one family in Queensland have been found to have leprosy. They include the father and sons and daughters. They have all been moved to a **lazarette** on Peel Island. The previous highest number in Queensland was five for a white family, and five for a black family.

SEPTEMBER NEWS ITEMS

The **worlds' speed record** for planes was broken when a British RAF Meteor flew at **a speed of 626 miles per hour.**

The new **basic wage for women will be 75 per cent of the male wage**. There is as yet no mention of "for equivalent work". Still, the International Labour Office is saying that "equal pay for equal work" is inevitable....

The idea that the man of the family is the sole breadwinner, and should get more pay, is dying a slow death, says the ILO.

Federal elections were getting close. So candidates were making promises about how good they will be if they get elected. One interesting promise came from **Arthur Fadden, the Leader of the Country Party. If elected, he would deport all Communists....**

Of course, this is just so much hot air. He is secure in the knowledge that if he is re-elected (he was) his Party is only the **junior partner in a coalition** with the Liberals. Happily, he could then say, "I tried to eject them, but I was out-voted...."

He went on to say that, as a would-be Treasurer, **he would reduce income tax by 28 per** cent. **Whacko. That's a lot.** Surely, **this** is not **more** hot air.

Nine women and 52 men were put into police paddy wagons and then charged at a Sydney court. **They had been caught at a baccarat school, where bets running into thousands of pounds were executed**. Those charged included professional men, and racing identities. Some of the women, well dressed, became hysterical as they were removed from premises....

The next night, 115 men were arrested in three suburbs for playing two-up. Then 162 the next night. Floating illegal gambling games were endemic right round the nation. Police Flying Squads tried to keep up with them as that kept changing their premises....

A week later, police caught 12 gamblers in a two-up raid **at Rookwood cemetery**. Fifty others escaped by running through the tombstones into the bush. The gambling ring was lit by a circle of lanterns, and heated by kerosene stoves.

In London, 1,000 squatters moved in on luxury vacant flats in Kensington. The occupation was well planned, and the 400 families completed it in 10 minutes. London authorities have immediately issued writs against all involved.

Two days later, the army vacated a military hospital in Holland Park in **Queensland.** Truck loads of squatters moved in, only to realise that water and electricity had been cut off. **The Minister for the Army, past Prime Minister Forde**, was notified, and he ordered the restoration of services. He said **"I have the greatest sympathy for homeless families."** It was generally agreed that his comment should not be seen as **an encouragement for trespassers to break the law**.

Commonwealth Disposals will sell **military aircraft to the value of 29 million Pounds**. Magnificent Catalina flying machines will go for 1,000 Pounds each.

ELECTIONS

National elections were held at the end of September. The only two serious contenders for power were **the Labour Party**, led by Ben Chifley, and **the Liberal**s, led by Bob Menzies. A few months before, **in Britain**, the standing Prime Minister, **Winston Churchill, had been beaten** at similar national polls by the Labour Government of Clement Attlee, and it seemed to some observers that this **display of ingratitude to the war-time leader** might be repeated in Australia. But this was not to be, and Chifley was returned with a comfortable majority in both Houses of Parliament.

The election campaign was vigorous. You should remember that candidates in those days **stumped** round the nation, holding public meetings in town halls and football grounds, before large crowds of supporters and hecklers. It was all much more civilized that the sanitised campaigns of today, with the wanna-be's sitting talking so smoothly into TV cameras, to a vast audience that is watching something else. In this case, both the leaders took and gave a lot of very direct abuse, and this did not seem to worry either.

Their campaigns were based, to a large extent, on the past. In particular, on who had done what in the war years. Even now, the nation was not ready to look forward to grand schemes for national development, and instead was caught up with the devolution from war. Chifley was able to say that, in government, he was in the process of introducing the welfare state, and for this he did get some net credit.

Supplementing this, there was still the distrust of Menzies. He had been sacked by the nation in 1940, early in the War. Then, as Prime Minister, he had supported the export of "pig iron" to Japan, at a time when that nation was becoming increasingly bellicose. He was accused by many people of giving them materials that were later returned in the form of bombs. Now, the appellation "Pig Iron Bob" was one that voters remembered, and it haunted him throughout the campaign.

Menzies also missed the plot when he did not exploit the growing sore point of rationing. Instead, he supported rationing, and even advocated imposing stricter quotas. Though, I point out, when it came to the 1949 elections, he had changed his tune. The very first thing he did **then**, after becoming Prime Minister, was repeal petrol rationing – which was the cross on which Chifley was then crucified.

The following reports give some highlights of the campaign.

News item, September 12. Police arrested 12 men during a riotous meeting at Darlinghurst, last night, where the leader of the Opposition, Mr. Menzies was the principal speaker. Many other interjectors were removed from the hall. Linen bags containing lumps of iron were thrown at Mr. Menzies, who was supporting the Liberal candidate for East Sydney – the seat now held by the firebrand Minister for Labor, Eddie Ward. The wires to the amplifying system were cut inside and outside the hall. Menzies was booed, counted-out, and jeered constantly. Early speakers at the meeting were subjected to almost continuous interruption by a big group of men and women, who at one stage rose and sang "Solidarity for Ever."

A number of women at the front of the crowd became hysterical, and were shepherded out. When technicians were called to repair the wires, Mr. Menzies stood at the front of the platform smiling at the hostile crowd. When he had been counted out time after time, he unhurriedly raised a glass of water with the comment "I drink to Eddie's (Ward) communist friends."

One flung bag of iron went near his head, and made him duck. He extracted a piece of iron, and put it in his pocket, with the remark "This will do as a souvenir." A man advanced threateningly up the hall and fought madly when police approached. It took nine policemen to throw him out of the hall. A woman wearing a red cloak appeared on one of the Press tables, and when police advanced towards her, supporters carried her back on their upturned hands until she was out of police range. All the time the crowd was shouting "Pig Iron Bob."

Press report, Sept 22, Hobart: The leader of the Opposition, Mr. Menzies, exchanged sallies with interjectors at a crowded meeting in the Hobart Town Hall.

Mr. Menzies did not pull his punches when he replied to interjectors. One man he called a silly prawn. He told another "poor fish" that his government would willingly give financial aid to special classes for backward adults like him.

More than 3,000 people gave Mr. Menzies an enthusiastic welcome, cheering and **waving hats** in the air when he came onto the platform. Sustained clapping lasted two minutes, while booing that broke out in small pockets in the crowd was drowned out by more cheering and clapping. He drew more applause when he described a man as a "red-faced yahoo."

Mr. Menzies was given a remarkable ovation at the conclusion of his address.

News report, Sept 23: Electioneering was conducted in a quieter spirit yesterday after the uproarious meeting which the leader of the Opposition tried to address at Darlinghurst on Monday night. The Prime Minister, Mr. Chifley, addressed an enthusiastic and overflowing audience of 2,500 in the Adelaide Town Hall last night.

Mr. Chifley again recited the history of the collapse of the Menzies and Fadden governments. He said that these governments had fallen, not by any action from the Labor Party, but because Mr. Menzies' supporters had regarded him as being too futile to occupy the top job. Labour had come to power when the country was practically defenceless. It organized for war, sought aid from America, and geared the nation's economy for war. Labor had provided the leadership and organization, but the people of Australia were responsible for the war effort.

Australia had changed from the old days when governments went begging to private banks for loans. We had previously piled up huge debts overseas. Australia had reduced its overseas debt, while the war was actually on, by 72 million pounds, thereby reducing its interest bill by six million pounds per year.

Attacking Board control of the Commonwealth Bank during the depression years, Mr. Chifley said he did not know a more ghastly financial policy. The men controlling the banks were seven or eight big businessmen. Because of their training, and although they were completely honest, they were inhumane. Their idea was that as long as vested interests were protected, stability was achieved.

Men in their thousands fought at factory gates for a couple of jobs, and 750,000 workers with wives and families were workless. "The Labor Government would be dead to all sense of humane feeling if it did not see that such a state of circumstances did not occur again. The people of Australia should make up their minds that never again should Robert Menzies and those associated with him be permitted to place Australians under the thralldom of private interest."

Chifley's no change policy.

Ben Chifley had served for less than half a term after the death of John Curtin in 1945. When he came to this election, he simply **stood on the policy of maintaining the status quo**, with the confidence that the electorate would not expect too much from someone so appointed. But, **jumping ahead to 1949**, he tried the same policy, almost making a virtue of standing on his performance, and not promoting major changes. Menzies had by then found Communists under beds, and in particular, exploited the fact that war-time rationing was still in place.

WHERE'S THE BEEF?

The ration of meat in 1946 was about 800 grams per week for an adult. That was not enough to feed a hungry waterside worker, or even a bank clerk. In those days, steak and eggs and sausages were standard fare for the evening meal, chops and cutlets provided a nice alternative, and Sundays were just not Sundays without the leg of lamb. Even small eaters felt restricted, with only half a pound of mince, and two thick sausages each week. The tragedy was that – in those days before diets and salads – the community was geared to eating meat in the evenings, every evening, and also to a large extent at breakfast. This type of restriction was tough to swallow.

Remember that **chicken was then a rarity** to be eaten only at Christmas and Easter. The many people who had poultry in the backyard got their taste of luxury a bit more often. But the limit was eighteen chooks, and this was tightly policed by special inspectors who took positive delight in prosecuting. Of course, there was no Kentucky Fried. Nor McDonalds. No fast food chains at all. Coke was just coming on to the scene. Was it possible to live under these conditions?

Apparently so. With the help of one type of meat that got through authority's guard, namely **the humble rabbit**. A thriving trade developed in these edible vermin. Rabbits were delivered in horse-pulled drays moving from house to house, where their nicely skinned bodies were flung in pairs directly into the ice chest in the kitchen. It was often possible to order clothes-props from the same rabbito.

Another solution for the beleagured housewife was the black market, which by 1946 was very sophisticated. By then, anyone who had the money could buy extra meats, or buy special cuts supposedly not available. Governments and Associations spent endless time fulminating and chasing offenders, but by then the rabbit was out of the burrow, and the free market economy had a firm hold.

The Letter below shows another side to the meat problem. Apart from the shortage of meat, and apart from the black market, there were argument about the price that should be paid for it, and whether it could be home delivered. This Letter raises many of the issues that bedevilled discussion on this subject, and while it **does not do much to clarify the situation**, it does raise issues that were being argued right round the nation.

Letters, (Mrs) Elsie Morgan, Hawthorn. Prior to the war, the retail price of meat was based on the purchase price to the retailer, plus wages, &c., overhead and profit, included in which was the cost of delivery. When the delivery was cut out, there was no reduction in the retail price to the consuming public, as in all fairness there should have been. The retail price has steadily increased during the war years to cover any extra costs to the retailer, and in addition he has enjoyed extra profit, because he has been paid for a service he has not rendered, i.e., delivery of meat. Yet now the master butchers claim that they cannot reinstitute meat deliveries unless the price of that commodity is increased. Surely the Prices Commissioner will not agree to such an unjust demand.

And there are people who prefer to go to the shop for their meat who also deserve consideration. They have been compelled to pay for a service they have never enjoyed. In common fairness they should be able to purchase their meat at a lower price on a "cash-and-carry" basis, instead of being called on to pay twice for a service that is not rendered, if the price is increased as demanded by the master butchers.

Then there is this little piece from the newspapers to show had badly the meat shortages were affecting ordinary citizens.

If the police can find the person who suspended a dummy from the Harbour Bridge early yesterday, they will charge him with offensive behaviour. The sight of the dummy shocked early morning tram travellers, many of whom telephoned the police to report a man had hanged himself.

The dummy was attached to the end of a rope suspended from the steel safety fence. It was made with calico and rags stuffed with straw. It was wearing a man's frayed grey coat, black striped trousers, and a pair of women's old shoes. In the breast pocket of the coat was the following note: "Dear Mum, life's not worth living without meat.   Pixie."

The Government duly announced in July that pork would soon become available again for eating. This was nice, because all such **pork for four years had been shipped off** to parts far and wide, and none of it had graced Australian tables. The Government might have thought that the arrival of pork chops for evening meals would be a vote-winner, but perverse Letter-writers made it clear that a stronger thought was one of resentment against the denial in the first place.

NEWS AND VIEWS

An alternative to strikes. Isaac Isaacs was the first Australian-born Governor General. He had written articles recently that advocated that **workers should be given financial incentives to do their jobs better**. He saw this as an alternative to the strikes that were used to get better wages and conditions. Here is one person's response.

Letters, A D. The recent articles by Sir Isaac Isaacs command the respect due to the eminence of their writer, and it is the more regrettable therefore that on two extremely important industrial questions they contain comments which are incomplete. Perhaps no man in time of peace should be forced to work against his will, but surely equal freedom should be conceded to the man who wishes to work under the legal award conditions.

Strikes almost invariably deprive many, against their will, of their right to work, and force them to accept loss and hardship. The savage punishment meted out by the unions falls not only on those men who attempt to carry on, but also on their wives and families. Is it not even more unthinkable that we should continue to condone these lawless attacks on the rights of others?

In regard to Sir Isaac Isaacs's comment on the "incentive system," I would state that in many kinds of work it is **quite practicable** to combine the advantages of the minimum award wage, fixed according to the living standard determined by the law, with **additional**

payment for output above an agreed standard. It is well known that piece-work and other systems of payment by results have been abused in the past: it is a pity that it is not equally well recognised that times have changed vastly, and that, with the modern outlook and knowledge, the benefits of the system could be achieved in many sections of industry without its drawbacks. I have been connected with industry for many years, and believe that **most workers would welcome a fair system of payment by results**, and that the increased output would make possible the improved living standards which we all desire.

Comment. As I mention later in this book, this is the industrial approach that was working well in America. Australia, though, had opted for the British model that accepted confrontation as the route to a better world.

Transport not the problem. Various authorities were saying that the hunger problem in Europe and elsewhere was really a problem in logistics. Granted, they said, they we here have a lot more grain and food than elsewhere, but we can't offer more aid because of the shortage of shipping and the money to pay for it.

Not everyone could see the truth in this.

Letter, W Sutton. A recent Letter voiced the sentiments of many readers whose sense of humanity rises against the priority given to financing atom bomb experiments while almost half the world struggles against the direst want. What inertia paralyses our leaders that they cannot **divert money from avenues of destruction to channels of mercy?** As it is our money they handle, have Australians no power to see that some fraction of it is allocated to the sending of food ships abroad. We have an abundance of food, and could spare tons of flour by a light rationing of only one commodity – bread. If the people of Britain are faced with this proposal along with their many other privations, surely Australians could volunteer with bread rationing, instead of appearing thoughtlessly indifferent to the obvious waste everywhere of this single item of food.

For six years ships and planes have borne death and destruction to mankind. Must we now believe there is no transport to bear the staff of life and the very necessities of existence to our fellow men? If the generosity of private individuals, and not national effort, is the only means of contending with the ravages of a European famine, **why is such a niggardly proportion of shipping space available?** How long must the bitterly distressed countries be left without food parcels, which at best offer no more than a mere lifeline in a sea of trouble? Our emporiums display luxuries, and our barns burst with grain while people 72 flying hours away from us sink and die from hunger and exposure.

Police are on the look-out for an ex-police dog that has left a military camp at Sydney's Malabar. **The dog is well disposed towards persons in uniform, but attacks civilians.** It is an Alsatian, and answers to the name Tiger. It you see it, **do not approach it**, and ring Malabar Police.

OCTOBER NEWS ITEMS

A Council Roundup reported that the NSW Dairymans' Association registered a complaint that the large number of **back-yard cows** were endangering public health. They claim that the cows are kept in primitive conditions, and develope diseases, including TB, that will be passed on to the human population. Thus they should be banned.

One side-effect of milk rationing meant that **it was not possible to get cream for the ordinary householder**. To get permits for this precious commodity, a person needed to have TB, a duodenal or peptic ulcer, ulcerated collitis, or typhoid fever....

He also needed to **apply to a government address in writing in the nearest capital city**, and to enclose a medical certificate supporting his claim. Pregnancy was not regarded as a condition for which cream would be available. If approved, the lucky permit holders would then be eligible for one and a quarter pints of cream each fortnight, for the next two months.

Magpies in still-rustic Canberra had better behave. An officer of the Department of Interior has been licensed to shoot any that misbehave. He shoots about 25 each year, according to the latest statistics. He takes this action reluctantly when he gets serious complaints about magpies chasing small boys....

This happens during the magpies' nesting season. "Destroying their nests only makes them build again, and they become increasingly protective and doubly aggressive."

The NSW Trades and Labour Council was a body that brought together a number of unions in an effort to get unified policies on conditions and wages. You can get a measure of the **harmony and brotherhood** that existed from the fact that, at a meeting last night, the **president shouted "Order please" 167 times in 100 minutes.**

Don Bradman is dubious whether he will return to First Class cricket. The English side is now staring a tour of Australia, and it is hoped by all that he will come out of a war-inspired retirement. A good sign was that this week he did go to practice at the nets. **Footnote. He did return to the game**, and had another remarkable season. Can anyone else remember his 234 runs in Sydney with the volatile and brilliant Sid Barnes, also with 234 runs?

A popular radio event at the moment was a programme called **National Quiz**. In this, a team of eight intellectuals from each State vied against each other to answer some erudite questions. Members were asked questions, and the team **with the best score out of a possible sixteen was the winne**r. Very exciting stuff....

On October 22nd, Victoria won with a score of 16. They won a prize of 250 Pounds. NSW was next with 10, and Western Australia came in last with a score of 2....

Questions that NSW got wrong included:

Where was the Taj Mahal? **Answer:** Agra

Who was the Sage of Chelsea? **Answer:** Thomas Carlyle

Island where Shackleton was buried? **Answer:** South Georgia

What was a Scottish "kelpie"? **Answer:** a water sprite

How would you have done?

THE NUREMBERG TRIALS

Before dawn, on the morning of October 10, 1946, ten men were led from their cells at Nuremberg in Southern Germany. They proceeded to the prison gymnasium, and there they were hanged. Their corpses were transported to Dachau, which ironically had been used during the War for the execution of masses of Jews. There they were cremated in the ovens that had been previously reserved for the Jews. Their ashes were thrown into a small stream near Munich.

These men had all been senior figures in the running of the German war machine, and had been found guilty of various forms of war crime by the Nuremberg International Military Tribunal. The prosecuting nations were Britain, the US, France and Russia, who had set up an elaborate Tribunal to bring to trial all the most senior Germans officials that they could lay their hands on. In the first of these trials, ten persons out of 24 were hanged, and as a result of subsequent trials, dozens more were similarly executed.

Three years earlier, the four Allied powers had started to plan the trials. It was not at all certain that they should be turned into the grand spectacle that finally eventuated. Churchill earlier said that he favoured simply shooting the Nazi leaders without trial, the Russians said they should be first tried and then shot, wherever they might be. It was the US that proposed a single venue for everyone, with a military trial conducted with all the trimmings of civil cases. This view finally held sway, and the specially-renovated Palace of Justice in Nuremberg was chosen as the venue. Two hundred and fifty reporters were invited, about six hundred staff members were hired, and the world's first use of simultaneous translations (into four languages) was under way.

The charges brought against the defendants were that they had waged wars of aggression in violation of international treaties. Also that they had violated traditional laws of warfare, and committed crimes against humanity. A **new type of charge** was that they had actually **conspired** to do all these things, and this **was made retrospective back to the pre-war years**. This latter charge has remained controversial to this very day.

Also controversial was the defence that these men had only been **carrying out orders from above**, in this case Hitler himself. From this trial forward, this defence **has been dubiously admissible at law**, even though the perception of its validity remains high in the general community. Of course, this presents a problem for the man in the middle, because the Tribunal gave no indication of how anyone, ordered to act in Hitler's name, could decline to do so, and still remain at his post or even alive. In this case, the defendants had no legal or moral excuse because they did commit these crimes willfuly and with a gusto that rules out thoughts of simply following orders. But the general issue that remains for future years is the extent to which refusing to obey orders is practicable.

The specific charges brought against most of the men were extensive. Hans Frank, the Nazi ruler of Poland, was of the opinion that "the Jews are a race that has to be eliminated; whenever we catch one, it is his end". He also wrote, "I cannot eliminate all lice and Jews in only a single year." In December 1941, he estimated that Poland had a population of 2,500,000 Jews. Just over a year later, he bemoaned in his diary, "At the present time, we still have about 100,000 Jews in Poland."

The Russians on the Eastern Front also suffered. Marshal Keitel complained that though they had captured 3,600,000 prisoners of war, only a few hundred thousand were still fit enough to work. As it turned out, a large part of them had died, because of the hazards of the weather, or from starvation or disease. Where they could not keep up on forced marches because of hunger and starvation, they were shot before the eyes of the horrified population, and the corpses were left.

Otto Ohlendorf was a commander of a mobile killing squad. At a pre-trial questioning, he admitted that his squad killed 90,000 men, women and children. He had been issued with orders to totally exterminate the Jewish population. He was asked, "Including the children?" He replied, "Yes." "Were all the Jewish children murdered?' His answer was again a simple "Yes.".

The list of their collective crimes goes on and on, and left no doubt in the minds of the eight judges that most of them should be found guilty. Twelve were sentenced to be hanged, and ten of them actually were hanged. Goering (see later) committed suicide on the morning before the execution, and Bormann has never been captured. He was tried and convicted in absentia. Three were given life sentences, and four were given 10 to 20 years. Three were acquitted.

It is inevitable with any war-crimes trials that some persons will label them as "victor's trials", implying that justice was not done because the victors set all the rules, and often change existing rules to suit their own purposes. They also have the day-to-day control of the proceedings. Of course this charge is true here. After all, would anyone expect **the losers** to set the rules? Or, in reality, to bring war-crimes charges against the victors?

But that does not, in this case, mean that the results of the trials were unfair. Granted, no one even considered the possibility that the men found guilty would be acquitted. So in this sense, the trial from the beginning to end was a matter of no consequence. Yet there are virtually no persons who make the claim that the results were unfair, or that those convicted should have walked free. In the long run, Nuremberg served its purpose. **Firstly**, to exact punishment on the major criminals and satisfy the craving for vengeance in the souls of millions who had been tortured by these men. **Secondly**, to again signal to the world that crimes against humanity would not go unpunished – by the victors.

TWO VILLAINS WHO WERE TRIED

Herman Goering first distinguished himself in World War I as an ace pilot by shooting down 25 enemy planes, thereby earning himself two top military awards. In his days with Hitler, he reorganised the plain-clothes Prussian police as the Gestapo, setting up concentration camps for political and racial victims. As Commander-in-Chief of the Luftwaffe, he devised the policy of terror bombing of strategic cities such as Rotterdam and Coventry to intimidate civilian populations prior to invasion. He also distinguished himself by looting train-loads of stolen art treasures and sending them to his Prussian home.

Increasingly dependent on narcotics, his prestige began to wane, and he was deprived of all authority by Hitler in 1943. He was finally dismissed in 1945 after an unauthorised attempt to make peace with the Allies. Later in 1945, he attempted a palace revolution, and was condemned by Hitler to death; he escaped, only to be captured by US troops.

During the trial, he was regarded as the arch villain. Through it all, he remained truculent and cavalier, and "death by hanging" was seen by all as the inevitable judgement.

However, on the morning of the executions, when the guards came to his cell to get him, they found that he had committed suicide by cyanide poisoning.

Rudolf Hess was Hitler's deputy until 1941. In May of that year, he parachuted into Scotland, with the idea that he could somehow negotiate an end to the War with Britain. The British regarded him with deep suspicion, and he was held as a prisoner of war until the Nuremberg trials. There, he professed amnesia throughout and was sentenced to life imprisonment. He was sent to the Spandau prison in Berlin, and was its sole occupant from 1966 until 1987. Then at age 93, he committed suicide by choking himself with an electric wire.

TWO VILLAINS WHO WERE NOT TRIED

Adolf Hitler. On April 30, 1945, Hitler and Eva Braun were settled in their Berlin bunker. The Russians were advancing rapidly, and Hitler's driver was urging him to flee somehow to places like Argentina. Hitler would have none of it, having already made up his mind to commit suicide. Eva too had made that decision, and she was the first to go – by cyanamide poisoning.

Then Hitler picked up his Walther pistol and put its barrel to his right temple. He pulled the trigger, and was dead instantly. A few of his last-minute supporters staggered up four flights of stairs with the bodies, and out ten yards into the garden. There they were set alight with many dousings of petrol. In the evening, their charred remains were fitted into canvas, and placed in a shell hole, covered up with earth, and the soil was rammed firm with a wooden pole.

Joseph Goebbels. On the first of May, Goebbels made an unsuccessful attempt to negotiate a truce with the Russians.

Then he agreed with his wife to commit suicide. Frau Goebbels arranged for a dentist to administer morphine to her six children simply to make them sleepy, and then she placed an ampule of potassium cyanide into each child's mouth. Within minutes, they were all dead.

The Goebbels climbed the same flight of stairs that the Hitlers had been carried up. Two shots were fired by an SS orderly, and they were dead. Petrol was also poured over them, and they were ignited. The orderly and others returned to the bunker, and executed Hitler's last order – to set fire to the bunker.

At various times over the years, there have been claims that Hitler did not die in the bunker. However, there were about twenty eye-witnesses, some of them still living in 2007, who have stuck to their stories without exception. Stories to the contrary can be put into the same category as Elvis sightings.

REPORTS FROM THE TRIALS

Throughout 1946, reports of the Nuremburg trial were given every day in all of the newspapers. These reports were often mundane summaries of trivia such as squabbles among the prosecutors and between the accused; these were given only about six column inches in the papers. Other reports were truly shocking tales of mass murder and atrocities. These were given more space, but probably only 12 column inches. Further, they generated almost no comments in the form of Letters to the papers: nor did they come from Editorials. Any comments that were made came from public dignitaries and politicians. It seems that **the general public simply wanted to put all those episodes out of their minds. Everyone was war weary.** People had already been horrified by the War itself, and by the revelations of Belsen and of Auschwitz, and while it would be wrong to think they no longer cared, they simply did not want to dwell on such matters.

A few press clippings are instructive.

Alfred Rosenberg's Testimony. Alfred Rosenberg, "High Priest" of Nazi philosophy, admitted at the war crimes trials today that he had approved a programme for carrying off children from Russia and the Baltic states to Germany. It was a "process designed to destroy the biological potentiality of these people." These admissions were drawn out of Rosenberg by US prosecutor, Mr Thomas Dodd.

Rosenberg also admitted that he advocated a programme of starvation and mass evacuation of Russians in order to exploit that country to feed the Reich. Mr. Dodd read a letter written by Deputy Fuhrer Martin Bormann advocating contraception and abortion for conquered Slavs in order to reduce the population, "Let the people of Kiev starve, abolish vaccinations, health and education services for Slavs," the letter read. When asked about the slave labour programme, he said he was under the impression that importation of labour was being carried out **on a voluntary basis**.

Rudolf Hoess testimony. Press Report. The man who admitted ordering the killing of two and a half million people gave evidence at the War Crimes Tribunal today. He is Rudolf Hoess, commandant of Auschwitz concentration camp from 1940 to 1943.

Hoess said he had not kept notes of the number of people put to death, because this was forbidden. He admitted however, that Eichmann, the man responsible for collecting the men, women and children for extermination, had told him that the **sum was more than four million**. Hoess said that Himmler told him that Hitler had finally decided on the elimination of the Jews. Auschwitz had been selected because of its good railway communications, and the fact that the camp was isolated from towns and surrounded by an area which it was impossible to enter without a pass. The camp buildings were deeply buried in a wood. Two or three trains arrived every day, each bringing 2000 people to the camp.

Hoess described in a toneless voice how the unsuspecting victims for the gas chamber were told they were going to the showers. Everything was taken from them on arrival; then they went to their deaths immediately. Hoess said that when Himmler visited the camp in 1942, he watched the killing processes from beginning to end. He hung his head when an American prosecutor read his confession that two and a half million were exterminated in Auschwitz, and that half a million starved to death.

His confession also described improvements at the camp. For instance, the Treblinka camp used carbon monoxide gas for killing Warsaw Jews. This took longer than the special acid crystals used at Auschwitz. "It took us three to 15 minutes to kill people. We knew they were dead when the screaming stopped."

Another improvement was that while the victims at Treblinka knew they were going to be killed, at Auschwitz they did not. Women sometimes hid their children up their skirts, but the guards always found them. Babies were killed because they could not work. Special staff members removed rings from the fingers of the dead, and took gold fillings from their teeth.

Ribbentrop's Testimony. Reichminister Joachim von Ribbentrop squirmed under cross-examination through a day of too obvious evasions of complicity in the Nazis' war crimes.

One denial he used time and time again when shown records of his statements as Foreign Minister, which conflicted with his current testimony in the Court. "I was speaking diplomatically, and my words do not mean what they say" was how he met the situation. "You want us to assume that you were telling lies then, but that you tell the truth now?" Sir David asked scornfully. " Not lies" said Ribbentrop, "That was diplomacy."

In one of the most dramatic scenes the Tribunal has witnessed, the prosecutor unveiled a huge map of Germany and its concentration camps. Every camp was marked with a red dot, and the map was covered as with a poisonous rash. Ribbentrop was made to look for his own six country estates on the map, and particularly for his State residence at Fuschl, near Salsburg. He found it easily enough, for it was surrounded by a violent outbreak of dots marking the Mauthausen group of more than 30 concentration camps.

"I should like to say on my oath that I have heard the name Mauthausen for the first time in this Court", protested Ribbentrop. He added that he had only heard of Dachau as an old peoples' home for the Jews. "Look at that map" said Sir David, his voice bitter with scorn, "In Mauthausen alone there were more than 100,000 internees. You passed them every time you drove to Fuschl." Ribbontrop looked about him desperately. Then he half shouted across the courtroom: "That was entirely unknown to me." "Do you tell me that as a responsible Minister of the Nazi Government for seven and a half years, driving all over the country, you knew of only three concentration camps?" Sir David asked. "It may be amazing, but it is one hundred per cent true," Ribbentrop obviously lied.

One question that arises is whether the excesses committed by the top Nazis were restricted to them, or did soldiers of lower rank join in? One example is of a corporal willingly, with gusto, killing 1200 people. This does not mean he was the typical German soldier; there are many reported examples of German wartime gallantry. But it does show that a combination of hatred, vengeance, ambition, propaganda, all mixed up in some manner, perhaps overlaid on an initially disturbed mind, can lead to savagery beyond human understanding. We can only hope, for the future of mankind, that such outbreaks are mercifully rare.

Goering's Testimony; Commission Reports. "The most dramatic point in the war criminal trials so far was reached this afternoon when Herman Goering strode heavily across the courtroom into the witness box. The three hours cross-examination by the chief US prosecutor, Justice Jackson, was a virtual triumph for Goering. He did not make a single admission, and he took every available opportunity to score off his questioner.

"Justice Jackson may have had some subtle plan behind his questioning, but to most of us in court he seemed to be frequently nonplussed by Goering's idealistic defence of Nazi aims, and his bland justification of the Nazis' methods. Jackson suffered an early rebuff from the court when he sought to restrict Goering's answers to either "yes" or "no". The court found against Jackson, and he never recovered against an opponent with greater dialectical skill.

"It was no wonder that when the court adjourned and Goering rejoined his fellow defendants, they grinned delightedly and eagerly sought his hand to shake."

Not Just at Nuremburg: There were other trials conducted at very many points in Europe and Russia. Some of them involved only the shooting of Germans when the hostilities ceased. Other more formal trials were run, though there remains a distinct impression that often the result was known beforehand.

Washington, ARMY report. More than 15,000 minor war criminals have been listed, and by the end of the year the number tried will far exceed that number, and of these a very substantial number will have been found guilty. It should not be forgotten that the Russians have dealt with many thousands of criminals in their own way. Also, that in all the liberated countries a considerable number of criminals, were "liquidated" by terrible and immediate "popular justice", and that Allied soldiers when they first came upon the ghastly horrors of the concentration camps in Germany, often did not wait for the "law" to catch up with gaolers trapped at the scene of their iniquities.

Comment. What can anyone say? You might think that vengeance on bad people is a good thing, or you might say that it smacks of the bestiality that they have been charged with. **But the reality** is that millions of ordinary people had been the victims of heinous crimes that these Nazis committed, and there could never be any doubt that retribution would be demanded either in staged shows like Nuremburg or kangaroo courts in towns and villages across Europe. Anyone who thought it should be different was saying that they wanted humans to not only to **act** differently, but to **be** different. **They can't do this and still be human.**

NEWS AND VIEWS

One of **the hazards of the times for shipping and coastal areas** was that **mines, laid during the war**, were still floating about in their tens of thousands....

With **a large cyclone** expected soon in Queensland, it was expected that hundreds of mines would be **torn from their moorings** off the coast. It was considered likely that **a "black ban" be imposed on entry to all ports from Cairns to Bowen for a wee**k. Minesweepers were already on the job there, but these could not cover the entire distance.

The war is over.   One exciting benefit I got from the end of the war was the opening of Army Disposal Stores.   Our national leaders were suddenly anxious to convert all the left-over materials into money.   So they opened stores all over the nation that were licenced to sell almost anything.

As a 12-year-old, I could walk into such a wonderland and buy military clothing, including the enticing jungle greens, berets, round helmets, slouch hats, and rising sun badges. If I had been a few years older, or if my Dad knew the shop-owner, I could add a few .303 rifles with 500 bullets.

For the big spenders there were Army motor bikes, trucks, jeeps, and camoflage nets. For the big eaters, there were cans of preserved food, including the succulent Spam and bully beef. And tinned biscuits.

What a place to spend your life.

NOVEMBER NEWS ITEMS

A 13-year-old boy, **attacked by a magpie, died** in Kempsey hospital from head injuries. As he fought for his life, several planes tried to ferry anti-tetanus serum to help him from other hospitals, but they all failed due to unusual circumstances.

The Melbourne Cup was run again this year, as it has been every year since 1861. It even ran in the WWII years, when other major events in sports like cricket and Rugby League were cancelled. You might think that people would be sick of it by now, but instead 100,000 turned out in their best clobber again, and boozed and gambled, and some of them cheered *Russia* (the winner; certainly not the nation), all the way.

A circus tent collapsed on a crowd at Temora in NSW. No one was hurt, but it took 30 minutes to drag out some of the spectators. **This should remind us that one or more circuses visited most large towns** in the nation every year, and that **crowds flocked to them**. These were the days when **lions and tigers** threatened to kill the trainers, when **elephants** sprayed water at the crowds, when **monkeys** were almost human, when trapezists swung without a net, and when **clowns** threw buckets of sawdust all over the place....

I know. I know. It's rough on the animals. It's fair enough that they can't be treated like that in Australia today. But I bet that **if an old-fashioned circus toured the nation now, it would play to full houses every night**.

The English cricket team is now working its way across Australia to start the First Test in Brisbane in a few weeks.

This is the first visit since before the war, **and its every move on and off the field is reported**....

The *SMH* is making its contribution to the excitement by **running a competition**. Readers are invited to enter by naming the Australian team that will be picked, and present it in batting order. Winners will share half the total entry fees, and the other half will go to a hospital. Entries close on November 20th , **so be quick**.

There was another round of the **National Quiz** conducted and again Victoria won. **Unanswered questions** included:

When does Halley's comet appear? **A:** Every 77 years.

Which woman's age was given in the Bible? **A:** Sarah

What is a Bunyip Peerage? **A:** One proposed by W C Wentworth.

The newly elected Labor government brought down a fresh budget. It did not alter direct taxation, but it brought down **a welcome reduction in sales tax**. In particular, it removed an **extra sales tax 10 per cent on all goods imported into the country. Clothing is now free from any sales tax**, if you have the coupons to buy it.

In another sign that the war is over, Chifley announced that **100 classes of war-time regulations will be removed** on December 31st. He noted that **60 classes will be retained**. Observers said that he kept control over such things as rents, land sales, capital issues and wage pegging. They said that **these were probably the most important issues for ordinary people**, and they hoped that relief would soon come from these regulations as well.

WE WERE THE RATS

In April, the heavy foot of the law descended on Lawson Glassop. He was a writer who had produced a book, a novel entitled "*We Were the Rats*", which inter alia tells of the experiences of diggers on the war front in Tobruk. This straightforward narrative, one of the best books of the nineteen forties, ran foul of both the NSW State and the Federal law, and its publisher was hauled before the courts a number of times to answer for its offences to public decency.

It seems that a number of government bodies thought that the words used in the book, and some of the sexual matters discussed, would give affront to right-minded people. Foremost amongst these censors was the Chief Secretary's Department of NSW, and the Federal Customs Bureau. They pursued the villains with considerable dedication, and managed to extract some minor fines from them. In all probability, the enormous publicity generated stimulated sales of the book, and from that point of view, the exercise was self-defeating.

Looking back from the year 2016, and considering the sorts of material now available to readers, and to viewers of films and television, the book seems in no way offensive. There were two thrusts to the prosecution's arguments. **Firstly**, the use of the word "bloody." **Secondly**, on two pages there was a discussion of sexual encounters in a frank manner, that would nowadays not raise an eyebrow in the Womens' Weekly. But they did **then,** and hence the prosecutions. The articles below show some of this.

Court reports. The chief police witness in the case against Angus and Robertson was Sergeant Roy Monroe who admitted in cross-examination that he was not sure whether Shakespeare's first name was William, had not read Bernard Shaw, and had never heard of Chaucer or Byron. Monroe said he was part of the Vice Squad, and part of his job was to look for obscene publications. He went on to say that five passages of the book were "offensive to delicacy and chastity." He did not know any of Noel Coward's works, and did not know that the word "bloody" frequently appeared in Coward's film "*In Which We Serve.*" He did not know the word "pornographic" and thought it might be a poor type of literature.

Mr Dovey, KC, for Angus and Robertson, submitted that the prosecution would make Australia the laughing stock of the literary world. "This is the twentieth century, and things that were once hardly whispered are spoken of openly today. There is nothing in the book that seeks to glorify pornography. It details only the natural reactions of the gallant men of the AIF".

Historical books like this one must be true to life. There are a few things in it which one would not place in the hands of children, but the book portrays in stark reality the fears, hates, and doubts of young men faced with the greatest crisis of their lives.

Unswayed by this eloquence, Sergeant Moulden, for the prosecution, said that because we were in the twentieth century was no reason why anything approaching lewdness should be published. Certain pages of the book were disgustingly filthy and offensive. Any person reading them would be offended. He added that **the word "bloody" was indeed indecent.**

Mr Farrington, SM, held that the book was obscene, and imposed a fine of 10 pounds, with eight shillings   costs.

This decision raised the ire of a large cross-section of the community.

The Acting State President of the RSL claimed that the verdict was the height of absurdity. "The book portrays the day-to-day life of Australian soldiers living under the constant strain of war. It would lose all realism if it were pruned to conform to schoolgirl standards. To object to the use of the word 'bloody' in a book about soldiers is ridiculous. If this attitude is maintained, much of the colour of our glorious war history will be lost to Australian literature."

The Chairman of Angus and Robertson, Mr Cousins, said "Where is our freedom? I do not want to enter into discussion of the decision about the book. Since June 1944, we have sold 10,000 copies of the book. Now we are told that after these 10,000 copies have been read, that our freedom was wrong. It is a staggering position."

Editorials were indignant. They said Sydney had been treated this week to the ludicrous spectacle of a sergeant of police, placed in the witness box for the purpose of prosecution, assuring the magistrate that he found a book written about soldiers of the AIF was "offensive to delicacy and chastity," in part because it contained the word "bloody." Whatever justification there may be for regarding the book obscene – and that is to be decided by the Court of Appeal – it is an absurd and dangerous system that tests it worth by the reactions of a police officer, the delicacy of whose mind may be due to the fact that **he is innocent of literary knowledge**. The only thing that can be said about such a prosecution was that it possessed the great merit of openness. The public knows what the authorities are trying to suppress; reasons must be given, and the opportunity is provided for evidence to be called in defence of the work in question.

This is far preferable to the suppression by the hidden hand of departmental censorship in the Customs Department. No reasons had been given for the ban, and even the booksellers were not permitted to know that a work had been prohibited (prior to import) until they sought to receive it through the Customs Department. The Minister possesses absolute discretion under the Customs Act to ban books which in his opinion are blasphemous, obscene or seditious. The formal rule laid out is "whether an average householder would accept the book in question as reading matter for the family," but this is subject to the Minister's judgement.

Lawson Glassop said that when he was planning the book, he of course considered just who his audience would be. He wondered whether he should pander to the wowsers by giving them a sanitised account of war, or whether we should confront them with the reality of it. He decided that reality was the only way to go, and that a pleasant account of war was not possible. "War is not a pretty thing, and I did not feel inclined to show it as such."

He went on to say that the banning of the book amazed him. He asked how it was possible that a book, already passed by the censor, could now be banned simply on the advice of an illiterate police sergeant. It had been in public circulation for seventeen months with no outcry. So why now was it in question? He added that Australia was now the laughing stock of the world.

Court of Appeals, Jun 14: Justice Studdert dismissed an appeal by Angus and Robertson against a judgement relating to the book, brought under the Indecent Publications Act of 1902.

His Honour pointed out that English law has always recognised that whatever outrages decency, or is offensive and disgusting, or is injurious to public morals by tending to corrupt the mind and destroy the love of decency, morality and good order, is a misdemeanour indictable at common law.....It is to be deplored that the author, who had no need to rely upon blasphemy or pornography to hold the attention of the reader, has thought it necessary or desirable to descend to both in the work I am now considering. It is my judgement that **three** pages in the book are just plain filth.....

Finally, I should like to refer to the **most objectionable feature of this book**. The dialogue from beginning to end teems with the **irreverent use of the name of the founder of Christianity**, and in a way that can only be a constant affront to the members of the Christian community. In my opinion, this book is obscene under the meaning of the Statute. The appeal is dismissed.

Glassop said that Justice Studdert has simply not understood the significance of those portions which he described as "just plain filth." Now, authors and publishers will be afraid to write or publish anything dealing with sex, and Australian literature will become innocuous.

Postscript: The Inspector Plods of literature were quite refreshed by their victory here, and continued on in their censorious way. They again featured as front-page news in 1948 when they moved against both *Love Me Sailor* and *Rusty Bugles*. Both of these were seriously undermining the very foundations of society by the use of "bloody", and were again seriously admonished by the law.

Of course, what seems **now** to have been heavy handed and somewhat laughable was not always so at the time. There were people then who were deeply distressed by swearing. Many religions considered it a sin, and most religions thought that discussion of sexual matters was replete with danger. No good man would swear in front of a woman, though in fact many a good woman would succumb to a forceful "bloody" when distressed. Still, for most people the prohibition on simple swearing was not justified, and the attempts to suppress it were, of course, doomed to failure. The good news is that Glassop lived through these travails, and survived into the early 1980's. His book is now regarded as a classic.

PIT WHISTLES (A Writer's Indulgence)

I lived the first eighteen years of my life at Abermain, a town of 2000 people in the centre of the Cessnock coalfields. Every man there was a miner, or a skipper, or a fettler, or a shiftman, or a wheeler, or something else to do with the mines. There were a few who worked on pit top, such as office workers, but these were seen as some form of lower life. And there were others, such as shop-keepers. These were acceptable, but never quite fitted in.

My strongest memory revolves around sirens. Pit whistles. Every pit had a siren that it used to signal all sorts of events. There was a siren sounding when each shift started and finished. There was a siren when falls of coal occurred in the mine. There were prolonged sirens when WWII ended. And every Friday, at 11o'clock, every pit in the area tested its siren for a minute to make sure it was working properly. Because there were a dozen mines in the area, and because each of them had a huge siren, when the wind was right, no one could talk.

But it is the siren associated with falls of coal that concerns me here. Any mine that suffered a fall immediately blew its siren, and kept it going for an hour. This was to alert the Rescue Services, and to soften up the miners' families to the inevitable suffering that some of them were in for. Early on at school, I remember that each time an unexpected siren sounded, I would listen to identify the pit where it was coming from, and heave a sigh of relief when it was not Abermain Number 3. But other kids, whose dads worked **that** pit, went home then and there.

My luck did not last long. One day I was sent home. And there I waited with my mother. There were virtually no cars in the coalfields then in the 1940's, so the dead, dying, maimed, and injured were packed into an old dray – otherwise used for delivering loads of coal to the miners' houses – behind a lethargic horse who strolled through the one-mile town to the victims' homes. We could see the cart coming for twenty minutes, we did not know who was on it, all the town was dead still – except for the sirens – and everyone was hoping that it was someone else's dad on the cart.

And so the cart came to our house and passed on. This was a huge relief to me, and my Mum's attention was now on helping with the grief of others. But falls of coal, and fires, and flooding, and explosions were always occurring in the pits, so that – inevitably – one day, the cart **did** stop at our house. Our first reaction was again one of relief because my Dad was still alive. We got him inside – onto the sofa in the lounge room – and found that, beneath the rough bandaging, his big toe and the one next to it were missing, and he had chunks of coal embedded in his soft flesh. He was covered in coal dust. His face, that someone had washed, was a colourless grey. Where his skin was visible, it was almost transparent, and I could see his arteries beneath it. He was sweating and at the same time shivering, in a state of complete shock – the miner working beside him had been killed. All the time, the Abermain No 3 siren was still blaring out   **Curse it.**

On two other occasions he was brought home like this. Each time his injury was worse. On the last occasion he had been crushed and buried for three hours. Over the course of six years in primary school, I saw eleven dead men taken past our house, and scores of others who survived for a time. And always to the tune of the sirens.

My eldest brother was 15 years older than me. He was tall, and slim, and manly, and beautiful. And he worked down a pit, so that eventually, he was caught in a fall. No horse and dray for me this time, because he now lived in a different town. But I knew his siren, and later that day we got the bad news. He was buried and they dug him out, and the pit doctor said he had brain damage. So he was sent to Broughton Hall in Sydney, a mental institution, now known to have been a torture-house. There he was given the famous "electric-shock" therapy. He escaped, and came home. We hid him from the police, medical people and mental inspectors until they gave up. He died, aged 65, with his lungs riddled with coal dust.

One good thing came out of all this: my Mum made me promise that I would never go down the pits, and that somehow I would get out of the coal fields. So I took the one and only path out by becoming a good scholar, and that eventually paid off for me.

As a post script, I mention that every Thursday at 11, the Eraring power station tests its siren. It's a skinny little siren, and I expect most people round here don't even notice it. But

I'm afraid I do. In fact, I set up routines so that I generally don't hear it. But sometimes I do: and then I feel sad and lonely; and angry. Because as I realise it now, the mines in those days were sure to get you. If you were not killed, or maimed and disfigured, there was the inevitability of getting dusted. My father was forced out of the mines in 1945, at the age of 46, and was never able to join the workforce again. For the next 19 years, he coughed up his lungs – sometimes actual bits of flesh – every morning for 15 minutes.

Then he died, still bewildered. He was robbed. So was I.

Now, an after-thought. One day, twenty years after Dad died, I was building a duck run at my small farm at Eraring. It was hot work digging, and lifting and carrying, so I took my shirt off, and hung it in the dappled shade. It was a green tartan shirt made of flannelette, that men from the bush love. It cost ten dollars from Lowes.

As I was cursing the timber and the wire, I was quietly thinking about this and that. Then, I remembered that Dad had worn a shirt like mine. I turned to look at it, and in a split second, in amongst the sun and shade, I thought Dad was there. It was a moment of rapture, absolute bliss. Then, immediately, I realised I was wrong, he was not there. He was gone, gone for good. He would never be back. I fell to my knees and wept bitterly.

THE ROLE OF RELIGION

Most of the population today accept as fact that religion plays a much smaller role in society than it used to. Church attendances are down, television each day **no longer** closes each channel with a blessing from the clergy, near nudity and swearing and violence are tolerated in cinemas and in the world around us. These and other signs of the "emancipation" from religion are now commonplace. Things have certainly changed from 1946. For example, **then**, all the Catholic schools and convents were staffed by clergy, whereas today, they are run by lay teachers.

Back in 1946, in a new world just starting to feel good about itself, religion took a beating. Mind you, it **still** had the power to control and affect the lives of a good part of the population, and its influence could be seen at weddings, and at deaths, and at christenings, to name a few. But things were starting to change; the resistance to religion was in its infancy, but was causing alarm. The following letters express some of this.

Letters, W Armstrong. You say that church pews are empty because of gabbling through prayers, perfunctory sermons, and overpowering choirs. Can anyone seriously believe that these are the true facts of the case? If they do, then their self delusion is to be marvelled at.

The dogmas and limitations of the church in the Middle Ages **will not, cannot, satisfy the awaking aspiring mind of present day humanity**. Dogmas may no longer hold pride of place, and hell fire no longer be thundered from the pulpit, but what is given to the people in their place to stir their souls? Vague generalisations and pathetic pious aspirations for the most parts.

When the churches have the courage and the vision to lay the axe to the root of the tree – when their dignitaries cast aside their limitations, their prejudices, and their fears – then, and only then, will saddened clerics no longer gaze at empty pews, for man is inherently good, and "the cry of the human heart is ever for that Divine life whence it sprung."

Letters, W Arthur. More men and women, but principally men, no longer believe in the fundamental doctrines on which the churches have built their ethical superstructures.

Putting it plainly, the virgin birth of Christ, the doctrine of the Trinity, the resurrection of Christ and his bodily ascent into heaven are less believable in an age in which reason is the test applied to postulates of all kinds, and not emotional "faith." The great power the churches might exercise by preaching the simple moral principles taught by Christ, they weaken by associating with them dogmas which reasoning man cannot accept, and they therefore are losing contact with those men whose minds have outgrown the limitations imposed by the churches.

The Rev Eastman, from the Presbyterian General Assembly, decried the status of religion in today's society. "Many people have lost the ability to think in religious terms. They should have the Gospel message proclaimed more often in their own language **with the aid of cinema**, where practicable."

Professor Haultain Brown (of the same Assembly) said only five per cent of the population was vitally concerned with doing Christian work. He suggested that religion required well-conceived publicity and team work. **Just as cricket and football teams visited various suburbs, so teams of spiritual advisers should visit the parishes.**

Comment. The drift away from religion appears to have continued. Here I am not just talking **only** about such measures as falling church attendances, but also the fact that religion has become more superficial, and that very few people have the slightest grasp of any form of theology or even the history of religion. Granted, in the past these subjects have stifled intelligent thought, and locked people into dogmatic ignorance.

So I report the change in attitudes to religion only as a fact, and leave it to others to say whether this is a good thing or not.

NEWS ITEM

In a tragic sequence of events, two schoolboys had a fight over a text-book, one of them landed a punch that stunned the other. The unconscious lad was dragged under a house, and in the process **he was strangled and died**. His parents and others searched actively for him for a week, until his body was found. **The other boy was charged with murder.**

DECEMBER NEWS ITEMS

I am able to report on the most important event of the year. **The First Cricket Test between Britain and Australia** started in Brisbane. Australia started badly, with 2 for 46. Then **the greatest man in the world, in all history, Don Bradman,** knocked out 187, and mere mortal Lindsay Hassett scored 128.

Australia went on to get almost 700, and the Poms were bowled out twice for about nothing. **The greatest win in the history of the game.** At least that is what one small boy from Abermain thought at the time. **That small boy can still remember the full score card from that match....**

But here's a worry. Australian fast bowler, Ray Lindwall, played the First Test with chicken-pox. He bowled very well, but still he will be in bed for the Second Test. Just prior to that match, **the entire Australian team, including managers, will be tested for the pox.** The Poms will be tested too, but because English poultry is different from our local chooks, they **will be tested for a different strain of the diseas**e.

Wool sold for 71 pence a pound at the Sydney auctions. **This was then a record**, and it was clear that prices would keep rising. Australia was about to have a ride on the sheeps' back. A few years later, in the early 1950's, during the Korean war, the price went to over 240 pence. A Pound a pound.

Government restrictions on share trading will be lifted from January 1ˢᵗ. For example, it had previously been decreed that **all purchases of shares had to be held for at least five months before they could be sold**. This would no longer be the case. **Also, options trading will be permitted.**

New ration books for food and clothing are to be issued early in December. It had been hoped that the requirements might have been relaxed at the same time. However, food **allocations remain unchanged**, and clothing had a few changes but the overall rations remained unchanged. That signalled that there would probably be no change in the next twelve months. **The war is over, isn't it?**

I know that some, rather strange, people are not interested in cricket, but I must mention one event that **any follower will remember for life.** In the Second Test at Sydney, both **Bradman and Barnes each scored 234 runs.** Bradman got out first, and most commentators say that **Barnes threw his wicket away** when **he** got to 234, so as not to eclipse the master. **In any case, what a day at Abermain.**

Rail concessions had been allowed to men in uniform during the war. Free travel on trains was one of the perks, and sometimes also on trams and buses. From January 1st, such concessions were no longer available in most States.

It is my sad duty to mar the holiday period by telling you that the **USA won back the Davis Cup** in the great period between Christmas and New Year. As you digest this, I can offer comfort by saying that **we beat the Poms in cricket by three games to nil**. It is *this* that we should **focus on, rather than a silly game of tennis.**

TOP OF THE POPS

Prisoner of Love	Perry Como
Five Minutes More	Frank Sinatra
Let It Snow	Vaughan Monroe
For Sentimental Reasons	Nat King Cole
To Each His Own	The Ink Spots
Huggin' and Chalkin'	Hoagy Carmichael
Laughing on the Outside	Dinah Shore
Personality	Johnny Mercer
Sioux City Sue	Bing Crosby
They Say it's Wonderful	Perry Como
You Won't be Satisfied	Doris Day

MOVIE HITS

The Best Years of our Lives	Frederic March
Henry V	Laurence Olivier
It's a Wonderful Life	James Stewart
The Razor's Edge	Clifton Webb
The Yearling	Gregory Peck
The Jolson Story	Jarry Parks
To Each His Own	Olivia de Havilland
Brief Encounter	Celia Johnson

RESISTANCE TO CHANGE

When I get to the last Chapter of a book, **I get excited, and usually I get off the fence** I have been so carefully sitting on, and for a few pages speak about matters that the year's events have brought to mind. So, here I am **letting rip** on **the slow pace of post-war reconstruction**. If you disagree, please pay no attention, and go on to the safer on-the-fence reading that follows.

In 1946, the whole nation was keen to get onto a truly post-war footing, and to get moving forward quickly. It seemed, though, that everything was taking too long. This was not just by coincidence, nor was it made necessary by circumstances. There were at least **three factors** working to keep things as they were.

The first was a big body of workers who had cushy jobs and who did not want to lose them. These were "the head-office wallahs" who had **not** been dragged into military service and who now had heaps of people whose lives they could influence. For example, they might be a group of public servants in Canberra who looked after sales of real estate. If you wanted to sell property during the war, you had to get Canberra's permission, and you can imagine how long that took and how many hoops you had to jump through. The good folk running that system clearly did not want to lose their jobs and status.

But when you look at it, there were hundreds, maybe thousands, of such groups policing some function, and keeping records. How many chooks did you have in your back yard? Did you have a radio licence? Was your son bigger than normal? Did you want a ration book, and did you have special needs, or perhaps a baby? Did you want to sell a car for its true value, or would you take the Government's paltry valuation?

For all of these, and hundreds of other matters, you needed permissions, and application forms, and information. That meant small armies of public servants had to deliberate, nitpick, decide and implement. It was the accumulation of these armies that was resistant to change, and who held enough power to delay moves toward a rapid escape from war-time bureaucracy.

The second was that **at the start of the war** this nation had, more or less, governmental and economic systems that practiced capitalism and followed free markets. That meant, **regulations were not too severe, and the individual had many freedoms. When the war came, that all changed**, and rules and regulations and constraints became dominant. As much as everyone resented these, it became obvious that they were necessary to mobilise the nation, and to get it producing everything we needed to fight the war.

When the war was over, the Labor Party looked at the war-time efficiencies that we had experienced, and thought it would be proper to retain the controls of the war years. Put very simplistically, they wanted to socialise the nation, and to control its activities. So, they were slow to remove rationing, they wanted to nationalise the airlines and the banks, they wanted to control rents and wages and the stock market. What they wanted was a nation that would pull together, under government guidance, and if that meant that some freedoms were lost, that was just the price that had to be paid for a better world.

But that brings me back to the **second factor** inhibiting change. **People who saw this vision did not want much**

innovation. Thus, they wanted a conservative, closeted population, soberly working for the good of the nation. Not the individual.

The third was what we would now call industrial relations. That is, the trade unions and the capitalist bosses were locked into a class war that defied all reason. Unlike America, which had already realised that co-operation between management and labour would bring benefits to both, **here** the only way forward was to magnify trivial issues into spiteful disputes. So that petty strikes were endemic, as we have seen this year.

As the years rolled on, profits and thus wages that could have been earned, were not earned. Importantly **entrepreneurs, both local and foreign, took their capital elsewher**e. The net result was that, in 1946, it took real courage for investors to take the industrial risk of investing in Australia. Holden took this risk, but others such as Nuffield said it was too risky. Mind you, he went back to England, and **there** turned out to be even worse.

THE MONARCHY AND THE POMS

The King of England and his family were quite important in Australia in 1946. Page after page of the women's magazines were devoted to them and all women gossiping over the backyard fence knew well the lineage of the major royals.

King George VI was soon to die, and his beautiful daughter, Elizabeth, was to succeed him. When she did this in 1953, this nation rose, almost as one, to express their devotion and their happiness for her. It was almost as if she were one of their **own** family. And they still felt this way about the Empire. True Blue, we were then. British to the core. …. Well…. almost.

There were a few cracks showing, and they would grow quickly in the next few years. But, apart from those, an undoubted force that would continue to shape this nation for at least a decade was **loyalty to the crown** and the "old country."

Since then, over the years, the Royal Family have had many adventures, and given us the odd surprise. But in the last 70-odd years, they have stuck it out in Britain, and it appears that they will still be there for many years to come. Here, in Australia, their future is uncertain, with the injection of the republican movement calling for their royal blood. Still, until the republicans can put up a truly viable alternative, it seems the royals will retain an address in Australia; and that will not worry most Australians too much.

What about the Poms? Of course, everyone in Australia was disappointed that rationing had survived the full year, and it looked certain to go on and on. The interesting thing is that, even now, there was so little serious or organized complaint about it. The War was over, promises had not been kept, and **yet there was no real rise in complaints**. The secret was that large and undoubtedly influential parts of the population thought of themselves as **British subjects** (which incidentally they still were), and this took equal place with their Australian self-interest. In other words, they were prepared to continue their current level of sacrifice in order to help complete strangers in the Old Country. **Because we were all British.** Then. **Things are a lot different now.**

SO WHAT'S CHANGED IN 70 YEARS?

I am sitting in a spacious air-conditioned unit with a good view in a nice middle-class suburb. I am surrounded by all mod cons, I have one or two cars in the air-conditioned garage, I can eat croissants and marmalade on a Sunday morning, and have a better wardrobe that I can possibly need.

If my parents had looked forward 80 years, from 1946, and seen me now, they would have been astounded. First of all at the material progress that has been made. TV, micro-waves, dishwashers, remote controls, down lights, the internet, YouTube, and the long list goes on.

But equally they would have been surprised by what had happened to me. I have more wealth, and I have had a life and adventures, that they could never have **imagined** possible. And I am nothing special. All of that is true for everyone around me. There is no way they could have comprehended the marvels that society has produced over 80 years.

But it works both ways. When I have moments of introspection and look back, I have sometimes come close to despair. How did Dad get up every morning six days a week, leave his hovel, and go down a pit? For 50 weeks a year, with the knowledge that he would do this till death? How did Mum get up to face washing day every Monday, ironing day every Tuesday, the week's shopping day every Thursday by bus to Cessnock, and cooking day every Sunday? Then there was the 4-kids-day every day.

She had no appliances, no toasters, no frig, no vacuum cleaner. She did have a copper, and a coal scuttle, and a chip heater, and we, and half the neighbours, had running water. Don't forget, in counting the blessings, the brick dunny in the back corner of the yard, in the opposite corner from the chook shed. Guess how many hens we had.

I, in my turn, can't **imagine** what kept them going. One thing that counted a lot was that we were a happy family. Another was that, though we were poor, no one else round us had assets or money. So the demon of envy never plagued us. We were just an internally contented family.

Another thing that doubtless comforted them was that we children were clearly on track to get out of the coalfields. We didn't have a champion greyhound dog, and we were no good at boxing, so we would have to find another way out. We didn't have the money for lottery tickets, so that avenue was not on. There was one other way. To study hard, and get a scholarship to Teachers' College, or maybe even to university. As I look back, I am happy to say that most of us children did that. That was always a comfort to my parents.

In any case, still 70 years later, I live in a different world from my parents in so many ways. I don't think they could fit into it all that easily, but I am sure that they would be delighted that this country has given me the opportunity to do what they had no chance of doing.

WHAT MUMS DID

One thing that Mum did was talk. Not to herself, and not just inside the house to the family, but to all the other mums round the place. She used to talk every afternoon across the side fence, to the Coats family, after she had finished milking the cow. And up the back fence to Tommy and Hannah, when we swapped our daily papers, the Daily Telegraph for the Newcastle Herald. But not to the family on the northern fence, because they were a bit too rough and horse crazy. And they swore and cursed and fought a lot.

Then there were the other ladies who walked up and down the street. No one had cars in those days, and there was no petrol anyway. So they all walked to the shops, past our place. And they all stopped and **talked,** both going and coming. My Mum seemed to catch most of them, most of the time. Not of course on Mondays, because that was washing day, and no one went to the shops much on Mondays. Likewise there was little traffic on Tuesdays, because that was ironing day. On other days, though, there were talkers everywhere, because, after all, the local shopping had to be done.

What did they talk about? A few years earlier, they surprisingly did not talk too much about the War. **Firstly,** because we got so little information from the authorities, who were as vigilant as ever to protect us from anything we needed to know. **Secondly**, because every mum knew that everyone else had so many raw spots caused by the War that it was better to avoid the topic. So instead they talked about falls in the pits and the strikes and the misery these caused. When they got tired of that, they just plain gossiped. About **other** people, of course. About that girl at Saturday night's dance. About Ambrose and his brothers punching up policemen in Cessnock. About the new Catholic priest not getting on too well with the old one, because the old one wanted to get on a lot better than the new one wanted.

It was great stuff. Nowadays, learned social commentators might say it was therapeutic, helping poverty-stricken women cope in face of the dangers that came with being a mine-worker's wife. They might be right, but I do not think so. It seems to me that women, mums all over Australia, were at it all the time. And they did it because it was good fun. And because it was made possible because there were no cars. And, no television to silence the active tongue.

So that must have been one fillip to what I see as **their drab life**. Then again, maybe someone will look back on me in 70 years time and say that I have a sterile life, and find reasons for deciding that. All I can say in response is that, just like my parents, it's the best that I can manage at the moment, so I **too** had best make the most of it.

SUMMING UP 1946

The refugee crisis in Europe set the far-away background for this nation. Over there, millions of wretched people had seen their homes destroyed, their family killed, their assets and property lost. They were on the move from one part of Europe to another, they were on foot carrying their few belonging and still had a thousand of miles to go. Food and water were hard to find, and when it became impossible, they died.

We were spared this horror, and did our bit by sending off tons and tons of food and clothing to the Brits. But this was a drop in the bucket when seen in the world-wide context, wherein **1946 should be seen as the year of famine and the refugee**.

Here, of course, we were more concerned with rationing, there were plenty of irritating strikes to frustrate us, the housing shortage was perhaps improving, and the jobs lottery for returned servicemen was going full swing. By the end of the year, everyone knew that the fabulous new world they had expected would be delayed, and they set a new date for its arrival. But few had given up on it.

While all this was happening, little people kept turning up in their mothers' beds, with no clothes on, and demanding in their charming ways to be fed. No one at the time was certain what caused this epidemic, they just knew that these infants kept arriving. First one, then two. Only at three did it generally stop.

Ultimately, the authorities worked out that it was because people were breeding, but they kept their silence, because talking of sex was still taboo. So it all went on for twenty years, and this extraordinary phenomenon was called the Baby Boom. It had an echo twenty years later, and together these entirely natural forces, mixed in with a heap of technology, and the changed social expectations, **changed the world just as effectively as the violent revolutionaries of old.**

So, if you were lucky enough to be born in 1946, I say to buckle your seat-belt, you are in for a ride. Granted it will not be a smooth ride, and indeed at times you will think you are going backwards. But forward you will go. At the end, you should be able to look round and truthfully say, with a few nostalgic regrets, that this is a different world, that the old one has served its purpose, and that the new one is ever so much better.

Make the most of it.

COMMENTS FROM READERS

Tom Lynch, Speers Point…..Some history writers make the mistake of trying to boost their authority by including graphs and charts all over the place. You on the other hand get a much better effect by saying things like "he made a pile". Or "every one worked hours longer that they should have, and felt like death warmed up at the end of the shift." I have seen other writers waste two pages of statistics painting the same picture as you did in a few words….

Barry Marr, Adelaide….you know that I am being facetious when I say that I wish the war had gone on for years longer so that you would have written more books about it…

Edna College, Auburn…. A few times I stopped and sobbed as you brought memories of the postman delivering letters, and the dread that ordinary people felt as he neared. How you captured those feelings yet kept your coverage from becoming maudlin or bogged down is a wonder to me….

Betty Kelly. Every time you seem to be getting serious you throw in a phrase or memory that lightens up the mood. In particular, in the war when you were describing the terrible carnage of Russian troops, for no reason, you ended with a ten line description of how aggrieved you felt and ended it with "apart from that, things are pretty good here". For me, it turned the unbearable into the bearable, and I went from feeling morbid and angry back to a normal human being….

Alan Davey, Brisbane….I particularly liked the light-hearted way you described the scenes at the airports as the American high-flying entertainers flew in. I had always seen the crowd behaviour as disgraceful, but your light-hearted description of it made me realise it was in fact harmless and just good fun….

MORE INFORMATION ON THESE BOOKS

Over the past 16 years the author, Ron Williams, has written this series of books that present a social history of Australia in the post-war period. They cover the period for 1939 to 1973 with one book for each year. Thus there are 35 books.

To capture the material for each book, the author, Ron Williams, worked his way through the Sydney Morning Herald and the Age/Argus day-by-day, and picked out the best stories, ideas and trivia. He then wrote them up into 180 pages of a year-book.

He writes in a direct conversational style, he has avoided statistics and charts, and has produced easily-read material that is entertaining, and instructive, and charming.

They are invaluable as gifts for birthdays, Christmas, and anniversaries, and for the oldies who are hard to buy for.

AVAILABLE AT ALL GOOD BOOK STORES AND NEWS AGENTS